Are you winning or losing? If your life is too chaotic, or too demanding, purposeless, or even going so well that you want to keep it that way — then *Fighting for Time* can help. Dr. David Cormack writes, "I have designed this book as an experience for you, an experience which will equip you to live your life in a manner which gives more times of confidence, more times of satisfaction, more times of peace and rest."

In these pages you will find a course in productive and effective living. Dr. Cormack provides the tools you need to:

- *Build your vision*
- *Plan your strategy*
- *Involve your team*
- *Overcome your enemy*
- *Review your progress*

Through charts, self-tests, learning scales, and training exercises, *Fighting for Time* will enable you to defeat the obstacles in your life that render you ineffective.

Fighting for Time

Fighting for Time

Dr. David Cormack

Power Books

FLEMING H. REVELL COMPANY
OLD TAPPAN, NEW JERSEY

Library of Congress Catalog-in-Publication Data

Cormack, David.
    Fighting for time.

    Rev. ed. of: Seconds away! © 1978.
    Includes index.
    1. Conduct of life. 2. Success. I. Cormack,
David. Seconds away! II. Title.
BJ1581.2.C66 1988   158'.1   87-28376
ISBN 0-8007-5268-6

Copyright © 1986 by David Cormack
Published by the Fleming H. Revell Company
Old Tappan, New Jersey 07675
Printed in the United States of America

To Edith, for our times on the highway

I wish to pay tribute to the many Christian leaders and writers who have influenced my use of time and, in particular, to colleagues and mentors in World Vision International and in MARC Europe.

There is left for myself then but one day in the week — today. Any man can fight the battles of today. Any woman can carry the burdens of just one day. Any man can resist the temptations of today.

Oh, friends, it is only when we wilfully add the burdens of those two awful eternities, yesterday and tomorrow, such burdens as only the mighty God can sustain, that we break down.

It isn't the experience of today that drives men mad. It is the remorse for something that happened yesterday and the dread of what tomorrow may disclose.[1]

Robert J Burdette

Contents

A Word from Your Coach

Welcome! and congratulations! The fact that you have picked up this book tells me a lot about you. If you decide to go the fifteen rounds in this training manual, I can say right now that YOU will discover a lot about yourself — your strengths, your potential, your priorities, your motivations and, perhaps the most important discovery of all, how you can live your life in a way that gives greater satisfaction, fulfilment and contentment. Big claims? Yes indeed, but then this is a heavy weight contest — you with all your undiscovered talent against a world that wants you to come a very poor second!

The Contest

Make no mistake about it: life is a contest; one in which there are real winners and, sadly, very real losers. In your life, I'm sure, there have been times when you have been winning and other times when you have been losing; times when you have felt strong and able to cope and also other times when life has seemed almost unbearable.

What has been the pattern of your life? Do you experience more ups than downs or vice versa? What is your situation right now? Are you winning or losing?

You don't need a degree in psychology or sociology to see that there are more losers than winners in this world. Nor, fortunately do you need to take such a degree in order to change your experience and alter the balance in your favour — though not at the expense of others. In fact, as your life becomes fuller and more satisfying, this will also benefit those around you.

This is a book for those who want to win and are also interested in others being winners, too.

The Requirements

Endless books have been written about what constitutes a fuller life, urging us to embrace this philosophy, eat that food, try this method of relaxation or that way of thinking. Many contribute to our understanding of ourselves, and have helpful ideas. The book that you now hold in your hand draws its wisdom from many such sources. The Christian faith is one such — first because the great majority of westerners are familiar with its principles and secondly because this faith is my own.

So what does it take to live a fuller life? It takes at least four things:

1. Determination
2. Skill
3. Effort
4. The right environment

This book will provide you with the skill. The determination and effort must come from yourself, for, after all is read and done, it is your life. It is you who will win or lose, be satisfied or frustrated; and it is you who will have to answer to your god for how you have lived. The right environment may be created by the application of the first three.

This text is more than just a book. I have designed it as an experience for you: one which will increase your chances of enjoying and making the most of your life.

I will be your coach and counsellor throughout the fifteen rounds of the fight. From the ringside, I will support you and give helpful tips as the fight proceeds. In between rounds, I will review with you your performance and together we will plan your tactics for the next stage of the contest.

Why a Fight?

'Why', you may ask, 'the analogy of the boxing ring?'

The answer is that I believe this to be an apt analogy. Boxing involves skill, determination and effort. Changing the way you live will not be easy. You will have to struggle against inner and outer forces which will militate against you and for you, as the boxer, there is the hope of victory as well as the joy and satisfaction of each success along the way; a hope to spur you on.

The idea that life is a struggle, calling for determination and endurance, is very much part of the Judaeo-Christian tradition on which for centuries our western laws and values have been based. People were often exhorted to fight and endure. Genius, it is said, is one per cent inspiration and ninety—nine per cent perspiration.

But today, sweat is unacceptable. 'No sweat' is an expression denoting effortless assurance, manliness and success. Consumer advertising, particularly, encourages us to expect a problem-free life, with all the 'good things' falling into our laps.

I believe such expectations to be false. It was Sir Isaac Newton who first articulated the law of physics that states that wherever you have one force, there will be another opposing one. This seems to me to be true in the realm of ordinary human experience, too. If you want to achieve anything, you will meet opposition. It seems true also that people are equipped to and can develop valuable qualities from struggling against difficulties and solving problems. All too often today opposition calls forth aggression, anger and violence instead of being channelled into worthwhile projects — such as learning to use time more effectively!

How Are You?

The thought of a struggle may tend to put you off; people can get hurt, but how is your life at present? Perhaps you are reading this because your life is too demanding, or too disorganised, or too pressurised or just not going anywhere — purposeless, disoriented, ineffective or inefficient. Can I ask you, Does it hurt? Does the disappointment of unfinished tasks hurt? Does the guilt of split loyalties hurt? Do the worries, concerns and constant frenzy of your life hurt? Does the fact that you fail hurt?

I can guess the answers! In our society the statistics reflect the degree of the hurt in more mental illness, rising suicide rates, increasing family breakdown, drug dependancy and abuse, escalating social violence and public disorder within our cities.

I wonder what your particular hurts are and how much they are affecting you. Would you be prepared to take some action to reduce the level of mental and physical anguish that you experience? You would? Then read on. Go the fifteen rounds. Endure because of the possibilities and the prize that lie before you.

The Prize

'What prize?' you may be asking. 'What will I get out of this book?'

Benefits will begin to accrue from Round One. As you read, as you apply, so your life will begin to take on a new shape, a new pattern. Your direction will become clearer, your progress will be more evident, you will feel more in control, and your confidence will rise as both your competence and success grow.

Are you ready? Are you determined? Then let me measure

you up for the fight. For we are all different. The skills that you develop during the fight will help you in your life. You are unique; so too is your experience and your situation. Hence, the need to check you out.

The Pre-fight Check List

On the following lines you will find a list of thirty-six statements. If any statement is often true for you, give yourself 20 points. If any statement is sometimes true of you, give yourself 10 points. If any statement is very rarely true of you, give yourself 5 points. If it is never true of you, then give yourself 0 points. Score yourself for all the statements. If you cannot make up your mind between 'often' or 'sometimes', or 'sometimes' and 'rarely', then give yourself the higher number of points. Indecisiveness causes us to waste valuable time!

Statement	Points
1. I feel that life is passing me by.	_____
2. I feel an absence of purpose in my life.	_____
3. I feel a sense of disappointment with my life.	_____
4. I feel my life has no sense of direction.	_____
Sub-total A	_____
5. I feel that my life is shaped by others.	_____
6. I am unclear about what I want to achieve in life.	_____
7. I don't set myself clear targets in all I do.	_____
8. I have a strong sense of being out of control.	_____
Sub-total B	_____

9. I live very much from day to day. _____

10. I feel that planning is a waste of time. _____

11. I feel that my life is full of uncertainties. _____

12. I feel that planning ahead restricts me. _____

Sub-total C _____

13. I have difficulties in deciding the best use of my time. _____

14. I lose track of my priorities. _____

15. I find it hard to concentrate. _____

16. I have conflicting demands on my time. _____

Sub-total D _____

17. I forget birthdays/anniversaries/ appointments. _____

18. I miss deadlines. _____

19. I rush to catch buses/planes/ trains. _____

20. I do not have enough time. _____

Sub-total E _____

How do you feel at this moment? Please write down how you feel.

I feel _____

_____

_____

_____

_____

_____

_____

Statement	Points	
21. I experience too many interruptions.	_____	
22. I seem to take on far too much work.	_____	
23. I have great difficulty in saying, 'No!'.	_____	
24. I often find myself with nothing to do.	_____	
Sub-total F		_____

25. I feel tired during the day.	_____	
26. I feel disheartened by my lack of progress.	_____	
27. I feel bored.	_____	
28. I feel under stress.	_____	
Sub-total G		_____

29. I put off difficult tasks/decisions.	_____	
30. I relax by watching TV.	_____	
31. I feel that I could do a lot more.	_____	
32. I wonder where all my time goes.	_____	
Sub-total H		_____

33. I seem to put a lot of effort in but get nowhere.	_____	
34. I have difficulty in sharing problems with others.	_____	
35. I have no time to reflect on what I am doing.	_____	
36. A feel that a lot of my time is wasted.	_____	
Sub-total R		_____

Now put your total number of points in this box and read on to see how you have done.

Pre-fight Check List Assessment

It is easy enough to work out that the higher your score the more and greater are your problems in managing your time and living a full and satisfying life, but I hope you have been honest with yourself, or at least as honest as you can be!

If you scored over 200 points, then full marks for being honest, but, oh dear, life is really quite difficult for you and for those around you. But a good coach always likes a good challenge! Some very early instructions for you. First, go no more than one round of this book per day, but not less than one round per week. Second, turn now to Round Ten, page 133, 'Involving Your Team'. Then, after completing that round, come back to this point and we will go ahead together.

If you scored 150 to 200 points, then this is the book for you! You can really look forward to improving your quality of life. Many people have come to grips with the problems you are encountering and are living richer, fuller lives as a result. You will find the fifteen rounds stimulating, enjoyable and very worthwhile.

If you scored 100 to 145 points — well done! This is an exceptional score. You will find many suggestions in this book which together with your own current skills will enrich your life. You may find it useful to consider selective reading. If you wish, please refer to the index of topics so that you can concentrate on those areas of your life in which you are least effective.

If you scored less than 100, then you could have written this book. Judging by your answers your life is well organised, you know where you are going and you are successful in almost everything you do. But read on, you have clearly a lot of potential for helping others.

Basic Skill Areas

Now let's look in more detail at your strengths and weaknesses. The 36 statements in the Pre-fight Check List cover the nine basic skill areas required to manage your time more effectively and hence live a more fulfilled life. The nine basic skill areas are as follows:—

1. To be able to create and describe a *vision* for your life.
2. To be able to translate that vision into clear *targets* consistent with your vision.
3. To be able to identify your *priorities* for action.
4. To be able to prepare and follow *plans* designed to lead to the achievement of your targets.

5. To be able to *organise* yourself and your environment.

6. To be able to *manage* the many demands on your time so that you do those things you should do.

7. To develop and maintain the *energy* to do those things which you want to.

8. To *act* according to your vision, plans and priorities.

This leaves us with one very special skill (9.), and that is the *skill of learning through reviewing*.

Don't be overwhelmed or dismayed by this list. You need more skills to drive a car! Round by round you will learn how to develop these skills. Pictures always help fix ideas in our minds. Look at the star diagram opposite. There are eight points corresponding to the first eight sections in the pre-fight check list. Please transfer your scores to the scales on the eight arms of the star.

The star shows your areas of strength, (the low scores) and your areas of weakness (the high scores). In the fifteen rounds of this book I will be helping you not only to overcome your weaknesses but also to build on your strengths.

Let's take a few more moments to understand these basic skills.

To manage your time effectively requires you to be able to engage in these nine basic life activities and you already have all the potential you need to be able to develop them successfully. As with all the powerful ideas in this world, these activities are simple yet they have the potential to change your life.

1 Develop a Vision

We all have dreams, desires to be different, wishes to change the way we are, hopes that one day our ship will come in and our lives will be transformed. These feelings live at the very heart of our being. Dreams like these have changed the course of history as men and women have translated these yearnings into visions for themselves and others. You need to develop a personal vision for your life if you are to live a quality life. If you have a vision already you will be able to test, sharpen and enlarge it as we examine the principles, practice and power of vision building together.

2 Set Clear Targets

A wise king, in observing his people, noticed that those with no

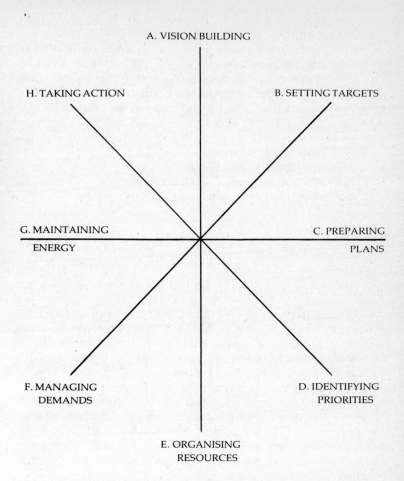

The Seconds Away! – Skills Star

vision wasted their lives. "They wither," was his sad comment.[2] He himself managed to rule a great kingdom, build some of the greatest structures this world has ever seen, write books, and attend eight hundred royal weddings — all of them his own!

Inevitably our bodies decay, but we must not confuse body and life. King Solomon was not saying, "If you have a vision, you will not grow old." Rather he was saying that people without a vision are old before their time. Compare two observations of the ageing process — the first by Shakespeare, the second by Browning.

> Last scene of all,
> That ends this strange eventful history,
> Is second childishness, and mere oblivion,
> Sans teeth, sans eyes, sans taste, sans everything.[3]

and

> Grow old along with me!
> The best is yet to be,
> The last of life, for which the first was made.[4]

Note that they are observations, not predictions. You may choose. If you drift, the words of Shakespeare can be your epitaph. There is, however, another way. You can enjoy a future which is not only fired by a vision but is sustained by goals — targets which you set for yourself and aim for — hopes, expectations, desires and longings which you have translated into clear statements of what you want to achieve. In Round Three we will come to grips with this simple yet powerful and enabling concept. In the context of this book, your short term target is to complete the fifteen rounds and to benefit from the experience. But a target without a plan is simply a tantalising frustration.

3 Establish Priorities

Priorities are those targets that we put first in our lives. Absence of priorities leads to confusion of activities — a continuous run from one task to another and back again. But this is not the main problem for busy people today — the real problem is that we experience a conflict of priorities. We have many important responsibilities and many urgent demands on our time. We must make choices: What should we do first? What should we leave undone? These questions cannot be adequately answered unless we have priorities based upon our targets and vision.

An added difficulty as we seek to gain control of our time is the fact that other people's priorities are not often the same as ours. What can be done when our career priorities come into direct confrontation with the domestic priorities of our partner? How do we deal with competition when our priorities are the same as, but not compatible with, those with whom we work? In Round Four I will introduce you to a simple way of setting priorities. This will help you identify what is really important in your life. Thus you may go ahead and prepare plans towards the achievement of your priorities rather than live your life according to other people's plans for you.

The same wise king who commented on the need for vision also observed that there was a time for every purpose, a right time and a wrong time for every activity.[5] In our pressurised modern society there seems little time to do anything let alone having the luxury of choosing when to do what we wish or have to do! So often what you do and when you do it is dictated by someone else or by circumstances over which you seem to have no control. You find yourself fitting in with someone else's priorities. No wonder your life is full of thwarted dreams and missed opportunities!

Demands on your time come from all sides — in the post, through the door, over the garden fence, via the telephone, the knock on the door, the shout from the bathroom, bedroom, kitchen, boss, staff, colleague, father, mother, child. No wonder you have no time! No time to think, to plan, to establish priorities, to get organised. Yet you have all the time there is. You have no less time than those who seem to achieve so much. You have the same twenty-four hours as everyone else in each day that you live. You have all the time in the world. So let us get it organised.

4 Prepare Plans
There may seem a world of difference between putting a man on the moon and putting a meal in the microwave but both require preparation, commitment, action and thought. For the moon, the preparation took nearly ten years; for the meal, it could take as little as ten minutes if the planning is well done. There are so many areas of your life that you do plan in detail — holidays, birthdays, anniversary celebrations, finances, major purchases and recreational activities. You have plans for your kitchen, you have plans for the winter programme of activities in the club, church, office, etc. So many parts of your life are planned, but usually each part is planned in isolation.

You need a plan for your life that recognises the totality of your existence, a plan that reflects your whole vision, a plan that reflects your whole being. Do you have such a plan?

It would be a strange house indeed which was designed by seven different architects planning in isolation! A meal prepared with no consultation by seven chefs in different kitchens, *could* be great but is more likely to be disastrous. Your fight for a more effective life needs to be planned well if you are to overcome the many challenges that you will meet. In Round Five we will develop your capacity to plan in such a way that your plans reflect the fact that you are a whole being — much more than just the sum of a number of parts.

5 Organise Resources

Those who make a success of their lives and those who make shipwreck, have the same hours to live and work or waste each day. In the classic Bible story the prodigal son who left the farm to go and live it up in the city, the wayward lad, had no fewer hours than did the obedient son who stayed at home, though increasingly the prodigal found more week left at the end of his money! The prodigal had plans, but they were short term plans. He had not organised his resources.[6]

To live life to the full requires you to put your life in order, to harness and organise all your resources — talents, gifts, experience, friends, family, home, possessions and time — to achieve your targets and priorities. At first sight this may seem a rather selfish approach, yet you cannot help others if you are unable to help yourself. So get organised!

Organisation is a basic feature of creation. Around us, no matter where we are, we see the power of organisation. You are probably sitting on a simple form of organisation at this moment — pieces of stick and fibre organised in such a way that they can support your weight. On your wrist is probably another witness to the power of organisation. Think of your body — a real miracle of organisation. The constituent chemicals which make up the human body could be purchased for a few pounds yet their real value is only appreciated when these simple chemicals are organised into the wonder that is you. The value of the paint on the canvas of the *Mona Lisa* is less than the cost of a gallon of petrol, but something happened when Leonardo da Vinci reorganised his raw materials! So it can be with your life. Those many seemingly meaningless, wasted hours, days and years can be transformed by organisation.

It is little wonder that we find ourselves unable to control a disjointed life. A life that is disorganised is impossible to manage effectively. If we have no vision, we can have no sense of direction or purpose; if we have no sense of purpose, we can have no targets or priorities, all our life will be made up of unconnected parts. We become locked in a circle of disorganisation.

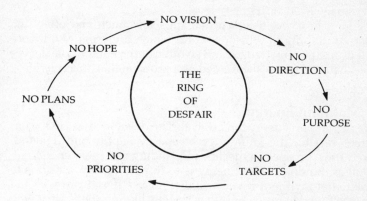

In Round Six we will develop the skills to break out of this ring of despair and discover the power of an organised life. When things are organised you can manage!

6 Manage the Demands

You know how easy it is to work in a situation which is organised. In some homes the butter is always in the fridge or on the table, in some garages the tools are always on the rack; in some bedrooms socks are always in the drawers, books in the bookcase and toys in the box; in some offices files are clearly labelled and available when required. We can all work in these ordered situations, but so often it seems that these homes, garages and offices belong to other people! So often our lives have to be lived out in that state of disorder in which spanners are in the fridge ('But Dad, the teacher said that things get smaller when they get colder and that spanner doesn't fit, so ...') or butter in the garage ('It makes the inner tube easier to put on, Mum. Look you can scrape the shavings off ...') and probably our homes resound with cries of 'Where's my shoe (tie, shirt, book)? I need it *now*!'

Readers gainfully employed outside the home may find just as much chaos at work.

Who can manage their world when it is in such disorder? Surprisingly the answer is, "Everyone!" Yes, everyone manages somehow, usually inefficiently, with a great deal of effort and stress. Somehow we all manage. But this is not the managing in the sense of being in charge of our life and situation; it's merely survival — keeping our heads above water. Not everyone is able to manage even at this basic level.

Living in a world which demands too much and offers too little or nothing in return, a world which undermines our confidence, saps our strength and so often at the end of a day leaves us exhausted and disheartened, is a problem that affects us all.

7 Maintain Energy

We depend on energy for survival. The developed world's economies rest on the knife edge of energy supply and demand. Countries prosper or decline depending on their energy resources. So do people. Energy is as important to you as it is to any nation: without it you will die; misuse it and you will find yourself unable to achieve your targets, like a trapeze artist who fails to grasp his partner's hands.

It's important to answer certain questions in relation to your energy. Have you enough energy? When do you feel most energetic? Are you a morning person or are you more efficient in the evening? When can you concentrate best? When do you feel most enthusiastic?

Just as time has its rhythms — day and night, summer and winter — so too you have your rhythms. You have probably come across the idea of bio-rhythms, as with many of these partial insights into human nature there are things that we can learn from the concept. For example, there are times when we are at a low physical ebb. This is true for everyone, although some are more affected by it than others. At such times, certain tasks may be beyond us, and it's as well to recognise this; otherwise we may put ourselves and others at risk. In Round Nine we shall consider some techniques for conserving energy and coping with times when we feel physically, mentally and spiritually low, but if you are in a trough at this moment, you might like to read Round Nine (page 113) before going any further.

8 Take Action

So far we have done a lot of thinking together, but this is a book about action, about doing and being, about changing and making things happen. Are you ready to begin to change the way you live? If you are uncertain or afraid of failure, then turn now to Round Twelve (page 149). Those who are ready for action, step this way: the weighing room awaits you.

> Rise! for the day is passing
> And you lie dreaming on;
> The others have buckled their armour,
> And forth to the fight have gone:
> A place in the ranks awaits you
> Each man has some part to play:
> The past and the future are nothing
> In the face of the stern today.[7]

The Weigh-In

It is important for you to enter this contest with the right attitude.

Recognise that each improvement is a victory in itself. As in the boxing ring every blow counts and every point contributes, so in your fight for effective use of time, every second well used is a cause for celebration.

In the boxing ring every good blow is cheered on by supporters but in the preparation phase for the fight there are no cheering crowds. No one sees the hours of dedicated training. No one is there to cheer the would-be victor through the weeks of diet, abstinence and psychological preparation – yet these are the disciplines necessary for success.

How can you be sure of success in your battle to gain more effective use of your time? Remember the four ingredients of success:–

1. Determination
2. Skill
3. Effort
4. The right environment

Skill you are already developing. You now have a better appreciation of your areas of strength and weakness. When testing some of my ideas for this book one manager wrote this to me 'Your first questionnaire showed me just how disorganised I was. I have really benefitted even before getting into the ring!' Determination will grow as you gain mastery over your time, and round by round you will discover ways to modify your environment. What is needed before you step into the ring for Round One is to ensure some early success. If you are a featherweight then no matter how good you are, no matter how well prepared you are, there is little hope for you if you try fifteen rounds with a heavyweight! You must match your tasks to your talent.

Gauging Your Weight

Are you a lightweight, a middleweight or a heavyweight? Before you rush to the bathroom scales for the answer I had better explain that I am not referring to your physical characteristics. I am thinking of your learning ability. Some people find learning easier than others. I am sure you are often amazed by the range of skills some people can acquire — languages, sports, hobbies, memory skills, creative and artistic skills. These are the people I call the heavyweight learners. Others are lightweight learners. Each skill they acquire, each ability and gift they develop, has cost them many hours of going over and over the simple basics of the discipline that they were trying to master. Learning for them is hard work.

Does the success of others dishearten you? Does progress seem so easy for others while you have to struggle to get the simplest of skills into your head? Do you always — or nearly always — seem to be last to pick up ideas? Occasionally, perhaps, things seem to click for you. Sometimes, (but, oh so rarely!) a book, or a teacher, seems to be on your wave-length and suddenly you find yourself able to grasp and do whatever is required.

To the astonishment of friends, fellow learners — and yourself, you can shout, 'Hey folks, look at me!'

I am sure that you will have had this pleasant experience — even if a long time ago.

Heavy Weight Learners Come in all Sizes

So, why is it that some people seem to be able to learn quicker than others?

One reason is that we all have different learning styles. Think about some different teaching styles: formal, informal, teach-yourself, and so on. They don't all work for everyone because people learn in different ways. The way that suits you best may not suit me best. One tutor or book may suit you; another may suit me.

Step forward now on to the learning scales so that I can weigh you. There's nothing judgemental about saying of someone, 'He is six foot tall,' just as there's nothing judgmental about saying someone is a light or heavyweight learner. Such information helps us to assign tasks in a more appropriate manner. To start with the heavyweight tasks when you are a lightweight learner would soon result in defeat and disappointment. On the other hand a lightweight task if you are a heavyweight learner will present no challenge and give no sense of achievement. So please place a tick in the box alongside the answer which applies to you in the questionnaire overleaf.

Score your answers according to this scale:

for each A: 1 point
for each B: 10 points
for each C: 15 points
for each D: 20 points

1. How many languages can you read?

   A One
   B Two
   C Three
   D More than three

2. How many times did you sit your driving test?

   A More than twice
   B Have not sat it
   C Twice
   D Once

3. How many books do you read in the course of a month?

   A One or less
   B Two
   C Three
   D Four or more

4. How many new sports have you experimented with in the last year?

   A None
   B One
   C Two
   D Three or more

5. How many DIY jobs have you completed in the last six months?

   A None
   B One
   C Two or three
   D Many

6. Do you go back to the same resort for your holidays?

   A Always
   B Often
   C Sometimes
   D Never

7. How many new friends have you made in the last year?

   A None
   B One
   C A few
   D Many

8. How many foreign countries have you visited in the last five years?

   A None
   B One or Two
   C Three or Four
   D Five or More

If you scored over 100 you are a heavyweight learner. You are interested by new situations, peoples and things. You make it your business to seek out challenges and opportunities. If you scored 50 to 100 you are a middleweight learner. You tend to specialise in topics which interest you. You are fairly set in your ways. If you scored below 50 you are a featherweight learner. For you, learning does not come easily — you have to work hard to master new areas. You find it very hard to change or develop new skills.

At the end of some rounds you will find interval exercises. Some of these are broken down into sections which correspond to learning weights. So if you are a middleweight learner, do the middleweight exercises.

As you progress with this book you may find that you can successfully carry out exercises at the heavier end of the scale. This is good, but please always *begin* with the training exercises for your learning weight.

Acknowledging Your Feelings

A number of developments which have contributed to making the world and our society the way it is today, have also caused many in western cultures to suppress their emotions. Fear is often concealed, anger suppressed, joy despised, and love is regarded as weakness. In his book *The Gift of Feeling*, Paul Tournier describes our technological society this way: 'Our Western civilisation is masculine and dominated by masculine values: cold objectivity, reason, power, efficiency and competition. This means the suppression of other values in the sphere of irrationality and subjectivity: sentiments, emotions and personal relationships.'[8]

From their education, many have received the impression that if something cannot be measured, then it does not exist.

Some religious and psychological teaching does not help us to live with and value our emotions. We are encouraged to deny, suppress or reject our feelings. Certainly it is not wise to rely on our feelings but it is foolish to ignore them.

When considering time management, feelings must be acknowledged; they do affect results. Many an examination has been failed because it was faced with feelings of failure and inadequacy. So also with time management. In his book, *Ordering Your Private World*, Gordon MacDonald confesses some of his own feelings as he faced the problem of putting his life in order: 'For me, the pursuit of internal organisation has been a lonely struggle because frankly, I have found there is almost a universal reluctance to be candid and practical about these affairs.'[9] It is important for us to be candid about our feelings, no matter what they are, because this helps us to get them more under our control and to use them to aid our understanding of ourselves.

In so many ways making more effective use of your time and your life is like a boxing match in that it demands motivation, energy and determination; but the difference lies in the fact that you are initially fighting against yourself. It is your life. You can choose when to try to improve it. You can choose when to step into the ring. You can choose when to throw the first punch, when to throw in the towel.

How do you feel? Ready to improve your life's effectiveness? If so, then come with me for Round One. If you don't feel ready to face the challenge of changing your life, then turn to Round Twelve — Healing your Hurts (page 149). Please read to the end of that chapter and do the exercises there before coming back, when you feel ready, to Round One.

Fighting for Time

Round One

Assessing Your Opposition

You have two main opponents in your fight for a more effective life. The first opponent is yourself; the second is every one else! You use your time and other people use your time. In this round we will assess just how much of your time your two enemies are wasting or using ineffectively.

Think for a moment about the nature of time. It is inelastic: no matter how the time seems to drag or fly, it always moves forward sixty seconds to the minute, sixty minutes to the hour. Time may *seem* to stand still when you gaze into the eyes of your beloved but of course it doesn't, for time cannot be stored or conserved. Most other resources can be. There are blood banks, grain stores, nest eggs for rainy days but no second safes, no minute mountains, and no day deposit schemes!

Time is non renewable: it self-destructs, whether we use it effectively or not! We have rechargeable batteries, refillable pens, part-exchange schemes for cars, cookers and carpets but no renewable minutes, no longer lasting seconds.

Time treats us all equally; it ticks by for rich and poor, sick and healthy alike. What is different for all of us is how we use time.

Few people are really aware of what they do with their time. Their days and weeks are divided routinely between work (house or office), shopping, gardening, leisure, etc. To really improve on your use of time it is essential for you to be very clear about your present use of time. Where does it go? How is it misused? Who misuses it?

Your Use of Time
So let us begin this contest by sizing up the opposition.

First yourself. Take yesterday and complete the following table. What were you doing at the time indicated? For whom were you doing it? (Yourself, the family, the boss, the committee, the neighbours?) Was it urgent? (Did it have to be done then?) Was it important? (What would have been the result of not doing it?) An extract of a completed table is given below. This may help you understand what is required.

Assessing the Opposition Analysis

Time	What was I doing	Who was it for	Urgent	Important
13.15	Having lunch	Me	No	Yes
13.30	Having lunch	Me	No	Yes
13.45	Having coffee	Me	No	No
14.00	Reading the paper	Me	No	No
14.15	Sleeping off lunch	Me	No	No
14.30	Sleeping off lunch	Me	No	No
14.45	On the phone	Me	No	Yes
15.00	Driving	Son	No	No
15.15	Watching football match	Son	No	No
15.30	Giving first aid	Daughter	Yes	Yes
15.45	Preparing fixture list	Club	No	Yes

An Example

This is an important exercise. Do not be tempted to move on without completing it. If you have no time to do it now, then decide when you will have time and commit yourself to doing it. A good time would be last thing this evening or first thing tomorrow morning. You will find it quicker to group times together if one activity took you more than fifteen minutes. For example 'lunch' may be spread over two time blocks.

Time	What was I doing	Who was it for?	Tick if urgent	Tick if important
06.00				
06.15				
06.30				
06.45				
07.00 etc 23.00				

Now let us have a look at how yesterday was spent:

1. How long was your waking day? _____hours
_____minutes

2. How much time did you spend doing things for:
yourself?_____ hours_____ minutes
others?_____ hours_____minutes

3. How much time did you spend doing non-urgent
things? _____ hours_____ minutes

4. How much time did you spend doing unimportant
things? _____ hours_____minutes

5. How satisfied do you feel about how you used
your time yesterday. Was it a 'good' day or a 'bad'
day in terms of how you feel you used your time?

Very Good _____ Yes/No
Good _____ Yes/No
Mixed _____ Yes/No
Bad _____ Yes/No
Very Bad _____ Yes/No

6. Was yesterday a typical day or was it different
(much better, or much worse than normal, or a holiday?)

A typical day _____ Yes/No

7. What would you like to change in the way you
used your time yesterday?

7.1 Reduce the length of my active day?   Yes/No
7.2 Increase the length of my active day?   Yes/No
7.3 Spend more time on myself?   Yes/No
7.4 Spend more time on others?   Yes/No
7.5 Tackle more items which are urgent?   Yes/No
7.6 Tackle fewer items which are urgent?   Yes/No
7.7 Tackle more items of importance?   Yes/No
7.8 Tackle fewer items of importance?   Yes/No
7.9 Feel more satisfied with my day?   Yes/No
7.10 Have a greater sense of purpose
    to my day?   Yes/No
7.11 Be able to sort out priorities?   Yes/No
7.12 Plan my time better?   Yes/No
7.13 Have fewer interruptions?   Yes/No
7.14 Feel less tired?   Yes/No
7.15 Put off fewer things?   Yes/No
7.16 Feel less pressurised?   Yes/No
7.17 Feel less guilty about my use of time?   Yes/No
7.18 Have more flexibility?   Yes/No
7.19 Have more structure?   Yes/No
7.20 (Write your own)_____

_____Yes/No

It has been said: Whatever you can do, or dream you can, begin it! Boldness has energy, power and magic in it. St Paul was a man who exemplified these words. He also knew how to be selective. Although he wrote, 'I can do everything through Jesus Christ who gives me strength,'[10] he didn't actually do everything. He selected what was important.

Now look at the list of things you would like to change. How many are there? Five? Ten? Fifteen? You may have in fact marked them all! High levels of dissatisfaction with how we use time are very common.

Don't be overwhelmed by a long list of things that you would like to change. The first step in changing things is to be aware of the need for change. Too often people regard change as a bad thing. Sometimes it is, but not often. In some situations change is vital to our very lives. Certainly there can be no improvement without change.

In this first round we have sought to size up the opposition — you and your level of awareness of the problems which you face as you move forward to a more effective way of living, and others in terms of how much time you spend on their needs and requirements.

The first round in any contest is always very draining. The competitors are nervous and wary and can become emotionally exhausted. Most fights are won psychologically in the early rounds. So let us leave the ring for a moment and prepare for Round Two. In preparation for the next round I have an exercise for you, whatever your learning weight.

Interval Training Exercise — All Weights

The Ojibway Indians have an evening ritual akin to evening prayers. Last thing before retiring they find a quiet spot and simply retell the events of the day to the Great Spirit. They begin with the earliest recollections of the day and progress through the hours, describing all events. They call this practice the 'everyday song'. If you are alone you may find it helpful (if a little strange) to recount your day aloud: alternatively you can go over the day's events in your mind — this may be just as effective and is certainly quicker and less embarrassing!

Do this exercise now and tonight when you retire to bed and repeat it each night for the next seven nights. It will do a number of things for you. Firstly, it will heighten your awareness of what you do with your time. Secondly, it will help you to identify what activities give you pleasure and satisfaction. Thirdly, it will help to relax you and improve your sleep pattern.

Try it now. Wherever you are close your eyes and in your mind go over every detail of your waking moments this day.

Round Two

Building Your Vision

Many people live without a sense of direction. This may arise from a philosophy of despair or from sheer thoughtlessness. Either way it leaves people at the mercy of their circumstances. A very different attitude is expressed in the following poem:

> Yesterday is but a Dream
> And Tomorrow is only a Vision;
> But Today well lived
> Makes every Yesterday a Dream of Happiness
> and every Tomorrow a Vision of Hope
> Look well, therefore, to this day![11]

Why are you still reading this book? What is it that you want to achieve? Stop for a moment and think about these questions. Can you answer them? Write down your answers by completing the following sentences:

1.   I am still reading this book because _____

_____

2.   By the time I have finished reading this book I hope I will _____

_____

Consider your two answers. Do they look forward or backward or both? Are your answers expressed in terms of yesterday's and today's problems ('I am still reading this book because my life and time is under pressure'), or are your answers expressed in terms of today's and tomorrow's opportunities ('I am still reading this book in order to make better use of my life')?

To live only to overcome today's or yesterday's problems is like running to catch the train that left 10 minutes ago – it takes a lot of energy; it looks as though you are making progress;

people admire your determination; but you are getting no-where! This book is about winning today's and tomorrow's battles, and this round about having a vision for the future.

What do you really want to do with your life?

Focusing on the Future

The story is told of the famous bishop who to his embarrass-ment lost his train ticket. Confronted by the friendly ticket inspector he searched all his pockets in a state of increasing agitation. Seeing his distress and recognising him to be a man of repute, the inspector tactfully suggested that it would be quite sufficient for the gentleman to give his name and address 'No! No!' exclaimed the bishop. 'I need my ticket: without it I don't know where I'm supposed to be going!'

Like the good bishop, increasing numbers of people in our society have lost their tickets. They do not know where they are going or why. Do you? Check your own sense of direction. Look again at your scores to the first few statements in the Pre-fight Check List page 15.

In this round we must come to grips with your future. Round One has prepared you for this so, although the issue of your life's purpose is a difficult one, you are in good shape to deal with it.

Pheobe Hesketh wrote some lines which capture the problem all of us face in relation to life — the tension between living in today's world and planning for tomorrow's. For her it was all too easy to become caught up in today's business and to lose her sense of direction.

> So man, conforming to his image of clay
> Is forced into ruts by the machine.
> Fixed upon a part
> How can he see the whole?
> Focused on a thread
> How can he see the pattern of a destiny?

Yes, too easily we become embedded in that rut — that narrow grave as long as our life. And how easily we lose our sense of perspective and become engrossed in the pain and suffering of our present distress. Our tomorrows become lost in the mist of our todays.

There are a number of reasons for this concentration on the present at the expense of the future. It happens to us because there are those in positions of power and influence who benefit from our increasing mesmerisation with this present world.

Think for a moment of the forces that have shaped your thinking. Advertising with its cult of immediate gratification urges us to take the waiting out of wanting now; live now, pay later. On a national scale, governments spend not only today's wealth but tomorrow's also, and the future of our children is mortgaged by today's leaders. All maritime nations have had a tradition of long term planning: oaks planted today provide the materials for the navies — in 300 years! Our predecessors laid plans which have enriched our lives, yet this generation has little or no conscience about laying down a heritage of nuclear waste which will last not 300 but 30,000 years!

The foreshortening of our horizons is tragically reflected in the pessimism of the young, 60 per cent of whom believe that nuclear war is inevitable.

How short are your horizons? Have you thought about what your tomorrows will bring? Have you a dream or a vision? The musical *Joseph and the Technicoloured Dreamcoat* contains a lyric that captures the need of our generation for a new dream:

> The world is waiting
> Still hesitating —
> Any dream will do.

The Value of Dreams

Martin Luther King, in his historical and classic address in Alabama, stirred the minds and hearts of his generation with the words, 'I have a dream.'[12] But today dreams are out of fashion; they mean change and change means threat for those who profit from the way things are.

Dreams have always been suspect. Those who had dreams were odd, different. Some 5,000 years ago, there was a young man who had dreams: Joseph. This story is written for us in the book of Genesis, chapters 37-49. His visions changed not only his own life but also that of his family and of the country in which he spent most of his life.

Dreamers live in today's world and look forward to tomorrow. To become a dreamer you need the capacity to imagine a world which is different, better. We often do this at the macro level and dream of a world free from war and want. Few people, however, focus on the closer-to-home dreams of a better life for themselves. I'm asking you to do that now.

For a start, write down five things which you would prefer to be removed from or reduced in your life, and five things which you would like more of in your life.

My life would be better if I had less:

1. _____
2. _____
3. _____
4. _____
5. _____

My life would be better if I had more:

1. _____
2. _____
3. _____
4. _____
5. _____

In Round One you began this process of building a vision although in that round the vision had to do with how you spend your time. In this round we are focusing on building a dream for your life — not just for how you might use your time to better effect.

If you have no dreams, you'll probably have no hope and without hope you are a candidate for depression and despair. But you are not one of these despairing people! After all, you are reading a book in the hope of improving your life. You must have a dream.

Obviously in speaking of dreams, I am referring not to your night-time dreams, but to your daydreams, your aims, targets, objectives, plans. Whatever you hope for in relation to your life, marriage, job, children's education, contribution to society ... can be part of your dream.

A Critical Point

Most people have their dreams in bed — and leave them there! That must not be your experience any longer. Dreams are for living, pursuing, achieving. First you must clarify your dreams, though this will not be easy for you. So far you have probably got by on the basis of vague notions about what was important to you and what you wanted to achieve. That must change. You cannot manage your time if you do not know what it is you are working towards. Besides, even if you were to become 60 per cent more efficient through reading this book, of what benefit would that be if you proceeded to waste the new-found time on activities which gave you no more satisfaction than before? You need to be very clear about what it is that you want to achieve.

So let's try to clarify your dreams now. Imagine that at the end of your life, your last word could be, 'Finished!', just as it was Jesus Christ's, on the Roman gallows.[13] He had accomplished what he had come to do. Now what would *you* have achieved in your life if that was to be your last word?

Think about this for a few moments, then write down your answer by completing the paragraph which begins:

My life would be complete if, before I die, I _____

_____

_____

What you have written is a dream statement. We will refine it later. This is a critical point in the fight. You cannot hope to stay on your feet in Round Three if you don't sort out your thinking in this area.

If you are stuck, read on. I'll try to make things clearer for you. In one of Jesus Christ's famous cameos or parables, he pictures a king dealing with his servants. Each comes before him and is rewarded according to his behaviour during the king's absence. To each of the first two servants the king says, 'Well done. You have been a good, faithful servant ...'[14] Imagine yourself on the receiving end of that commendation. To what things in your life might that 'Well done!' be referring?

Alternatively imagine that you have been granted three wishes for your life. What would they be? This is a very powerful question. You should not treat it lightly. Nor should you be afraid of the question as some people are. You have the rest of your life to live. Today is the last day before tomorrow. Prepare for it now by stating to the world and to yourself what it is that you really hope to accomplish. I wish the following for my life:

1. _____

2. _____

3. _____

Look again at your dream statements. How many elements are in it? If you chose the fairy godmother approach there will be three (you had three wishes — remember?) Otherwise, you might have one element or several in your dream. Your task now is to create five statements about your life's dream. If you already have three, add two more. If you have ten, then reduce them to five. Write these statements down as shown below:

My five life dreams are:	
1.	To
2.	To
3.	To
4.	To
5.	To

Now ask yourself the following questions for each of your dreams:

Yes/No

(i)   Is it really important to me?

(ii) Is it difficult but not impossible to realise?

(iii) Will it take me some time to achieve?

(iv) Will I be satisfied if I achieve it?

(v)   Is it a dream that is likely to last for me,
      i.e. be important when I am older?

If you can answer, 'Yes,' to all these questions for each of your dreams, then you have done well. If any of your answers were 'No,' then either rewrite the dream statement or replace it with another dream. Now ask yourself this question: (vi) Can I think of other dreams that I would like to achieve which are of greater value to me?

If you can answer 'Yes,' to this question then you are really doing well and you should replace one of your five dreams with this new one. If your answer is 'No' then don't worry, it is likely that the exercises at the end of this round will provide you with some more ideas for your future.

The Real Stuff of Visions

In a fascinating monograph on the subject of vision, Peter Brierley differentiates between the real stuff of visions and the unreal stuff of fantasy.[15] Visions are clear; they make distinct impressions on people; their effect is lasting; they cause people to change.

Check your list of life dreams again. Is each:

- clear?
- definite?
- lasting?
- requiring you to change?

If your answers are, 'Yes,' then I am impressed! If you have some 'No's' among your answers, then try to rewrite your dreams to conform more with the above criteria. Without these characteristics your dreams are in danger of being simply wishful thinking. With these characteristics your dreams become visions.

I cannot over emphasise the need for a clear vision for your life. The boxer will not endure unless he keeps his mind set on the prize which lies at the end of the conflict. A vision helps you to keep the present situation in perspective. Today may be tough, tomorrow may be even tougher, but with your eyes fixed on your vision you will endure.

A vision also provides you with direction. You have many choices to make in life. Without a vision how will you choose?

I was asked to advise a large church organisation on its structure. 'What do you want the church to do?' I asked. 'Have you a vision of where you want to be in ten years?' The blank looks gave me my answer. I said, 'I cannot advise you on your organisation until you know what you want that organisation to be and to do.' I am happy to say that the church has got down to the business of building its vision. One day I hope to return and advise them on their organisation!

A vision will also give you encouragement. Yes, there will be times when you fail or stumble; times when the opposition catches you unawares. At such times your vision will strengthen you. The late Sir Winston Churchill was a master vision builder. His graphic and moving speeches provided the vision for his nation during dark days.

Sharing Your Dream

Now that you have the elements of a vision for your life you should share them with others.

There are a number of reasons for this. Firstly, you will need to improve the clarity of your vision, and forcing yourself to describe it to someone will help you do this. Secondly, sharing your vision with others helps to build your commitment to it. Thirdly in sharing your vision with others, you are helping them think about their own lives.

With whom will you share your vision and when will you do it? You will find it easier to share your vision if you have it written down. Why not have it typed up and framed? You probably have plenty of photographs around the house and in albums representing your past — so why not frame the future? Are you ashamed of it? No? Then put it up where people can see it!

There are always risks involved in sharing your dreams — or anything else. For one thing, you might be proved wrong. But then you would be in good company. Simon Newcomb, the astronomer, wrote in 1903:

> The demonstration that no possible combination of known substances, known forms of machinery and known forms of force can be united in a practical machine by which man shall fly long distances through the air, seems to the writer as complete as it is possible for the demonstration of any physical fact to be.[16]

In 1945 during the build up to the testing of the first atomic bomb, Admiral William D Leaky said to the president of the United States of America, 'The bomb will never go off, and I speak as an expert in explosives'[17] — Boom! Boom!

So you could be wrong and people could laugh at you. Never mind. Take that risk. Share your vision, and don't be embarrassed by it.

Still fighting? Good. It is unfortunately true that many people never get their lives' visions articulated, so already you have shown yourself to be a person of some quality. You can be justly pleased with your performance. Step now to your corner for a break. We will use the interval to reinforce the gains made during the round.

Interval Training Exercise — All Weights

Too often we fail to use our creativity. Here is an exercise to help you think about your hopes for the future.

Complete this sentence in twenty different ways.
I hope

1._____

2._____

3._____

4.＿＿＿＿＿＿＿＿＿＿＿＿＿＿＿＿＿＿＿

5.＿＿＿＿＿＿＿＿＿＿＿＿＿＿＿＿＿＿＿

6.＿＿＿＿＿＿＿＿＿＿＿＿＿＿＿＿＿＿＿

7.＿＿＿＿＿＿＿＿＿＿＿＿＿＿＿＿＿＿＿

8.＿＿＿＿＿＿＿＿＿＿＿＿＿＿＿＿＿＿＿

9.＿＿＿＿＿＿＿＿＿＿＿＿＿＿＿＿＿＿＿

10.＿＿＿＿＿＿＿＿＿＿＿＿＿＿＿＿＿＿

11.＿＿＿＿＿＿＿＿＿＿＿＿＿＿＿＿＿＿

12.＿＿＿＿＿＿＿＿＿＿＿＿＿＿＿＿＿＿

13.＿＿＿＿＿＿＿＿＿＿＿＿＿＿＿＿＿＿

14.＿＿＿＿＿＿＿＿＿＿＿＿＿＿＿＿＿＿

15.＿＿＿＿＿＿＿＿＿＿＿＿＿＿＿＿＿＿

16.＿＿＿＿＿＿＿＿＿＿＿＿＿＿＿＿＿＿

17.＿＿＿＿＿＿＿＿＿＿＿＿＿＿＿＿＿＿

18.＿＿＿＿＿＿＿＿＿＿＿＿＿＿＿＿＿＿

19.＿＿＿＿＿＿＿＿＿＿＿＿＿＿＿＿＿＿

20.＿＿＿＿＿＿＿＿＿＿＿＿＿＿＿＿＿＿

Now return to your vision statements (page 44) and revise them in the light of the above exercise.

Round Three

Setting Your Targets

Welcome to Round Three! Are you fully awake? Remember, it is those who dream when they are awake who mean business in life. Are your dreams still clear? They are? Good. Now we can begin to make your dreams live. The last thing you want is to live in a vague and misty dream! The last two lines of this verse by John Oxenham capture the experience of too many people –

> To every man there openeth
> A way, ways and a way
> And the high soul climbs the high way
> And the low soul gropes the low
> While in between in the misty flats
> The rest drift to and fro.

Turning Dreams into Reality

Everyone has dreams. Few people realise them. What makes the difference between those who do realise their dreams and those who do not? The reason why most people fail to achieve their dreams is because they don't know how to set about achieving them. The dreams seem so big, so out-of-reach. It's all very well for the Chinese proverb to state, 'the journey of a thousand miles begins with the first step.' But what is the first step? How and where do you begin?

The answer is: Targets! They show us the first, and subsequent steps necessary for the realisation of our dreams.

A target is something we aim at. Aiming implies seeing the target – the bulls eye, clay pigeon, or whatever. It also implies measuring (How far is it? How fast is it moving? Do I have to allow for the wind, current or other factors?) and assessing (Did I hit it? How well did I do? What do I need to do to improve next time?)

The last question can't be asked in relation to your life! There won't be a next time so you had better get it right first time! And that is where targets can help you.

Someone who once came to see me had a dream which was: 'To have done the best by my family'. The many demands on his time — from business, charity work and his church had resulted in an unsatisfactory family life. He found it easier to say 'No time,' to his family than to the others who made demands on him. His dream — 'My life would be complete if before I die I could say that I have done the best by my family' — was a good one to have, but it haunted him because it seemed to be beyond his reach. He could not see how to achieve it; nor could he say how long it would take, or even what 'doing the best by his family' meant. His problem was that he had no targets. So I helped him establish some targets.

Asking the Right Questions

The translation of dreams into targets is not difficult. Just ask the questions, 'How will I know I am making progress?' Take the example of the manager with his dream of doing the best by his family — when I asked him this question about progress, he thought for a moment and said, 'Well, I'd be spending more time with my wife and I'd be doing things with the children and ...' There followed a long list of indicators of progress including more time at home, feeling less guilty about priorities, cancelling fewer family engagements and seeing the children take their place as mature citizens in society and the church. When he had finished I asked him to write this list down. Here is what he wrote —

1. Spending more time with my wife.
2. Doing more things with the children.
3. Spending more time at home.
4. Laughing more together.
5. Showing more love and affection.
6. Giving more support to each member.
7. Recognising each member as individuals.
8. Cancelling fewer family events.
9. Putting them first.
10. Preparing for their future.
11. Planning together.
12. Making more of birthdays and anniversaries.
13. Balancing their needs and mine.
14. Feeling that we are a family.
15. Feeling less guilty about my use of time.

16. Feeling less judgemental about their use of time.
17. Joining in their activities.
18. Having the family agree my priorities.
19. Learning something new together.
20. Going to new places together.

What that list did was to translate a dream into changes that he wanted to make. Do the same for *one* of your dreams, by asking the question, 'How will I know I am making progress?' listing your answers.

My dream is to _____

_____

and I will know I am making progress when

1._____

2._____

3._____

4._____

5._____

What you have now done is to build a series of bridges between your dream and your present world. These statements are not yet targets, but you are now ready to set up your targets.

Making Targets

Take each of your five statements above and quantify them. For example the manager's first indicator of progress was, 'I would be spending more time with my wife.' The questions now are 'How much more time and by when?' This caused the manager a bit of difficulty because I was asking him to commit himself — to make his dream measurable — to make it a target. Eventually he wrote his target as, 'To arrange my diary so that by June this year I will be spending two Fridays each month with Mary.'

Note that this really is a target: it is specific and precise, it is measurable and has a clear time frame.

The manager was able to come back and report that he had achieved his target by Easter — three months ahead of schedule. This particular target was only one in the set that was necessary for him to achieve his dream. He is still working on others.

Let's try to summarise the characteristics that all good, purposeful targets, whether long or short-term, have in common.

They are:

- written down
- desirable
- accomplishable
- specific
- precise
- measurable
- time related and
- capable of review

Here are a couple of target statements:

Example A. Target for my family life: 'To increase the time I spend with my son so that by the end of June this year we will be spending six hours a week together.'

Example B. Target for my work life: 'To reduce the amount of work that I bring home so that by Easter next year I spend not more than one hour per evening working at home.'

Both statements meet all criteria above. Now consider two more examples.

Example C. Target for my family life: 'To be a better parent.'

Example D. Target for my work life: 'To be more efficient.'

Notice that statements C and D do not meet all the criteria above. The deficiencies are obvious. How will you know if you have become a better parent or more efficient? These statements are too open-ended, too imprecise, to be of much help. The secret of progress is to set yourself clear targets against which you can measure your performance!

So — to work! Your immediate target is to write down in thirty minutes three target statements for each of the six life areas listed below. At least one of your target statements in each life area should be related to one of your dream statements. Therefore in the third column write the dream statement number against the appropriate target. The final column is headed 'Priority', leave this blank at the moment.

My Life Targets

Area	No	Target Statement	Priority
1. Family	1 2 3		
1a. Marriage	4 5 6		
2. Work	1 ·2 ·3		
3. Church	1 2 3		
4. Leisure	1 2 3		
5. Neighbours	1 2 3		
6. Self	1 2 3		

Interval Training Exercises

1. For heavyweight learners

Take a sheet of paper and produce a target tree. A target tree is like a family tree — it shows the relationships between individuals and generations. In the target tree your 'generations' are replaced by the levels, vision, dreams and targets. Here is one example of how you might set it up.

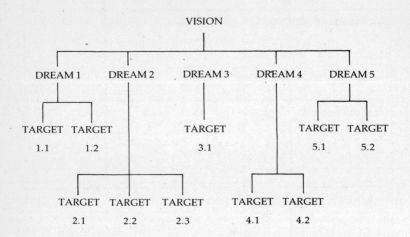

2. For middleweight learners

Look again at your target statements and your dreams. Have you set targets for all of your dreams? Have you set targets for which you have no dreams? Spend fifteen minutes making a closer match between your dreams and your targets.

3. For lightweight learners

Go back over your target statements to make sure each is a real target. Each statement should meet the criteria already mentioned (page 52).

Round Four
Identifying Your Priorities

As you begin to bring your own life together into a new coherent pattern, you will become increasingly aware of the disorganisation around you. In this round, while making progress with your vision, dreams and targets, we will introduce that second opponent – other people.

The Human Condition
We live in a divided world. At all levels of existence there is division. At the international level, East and West stand in seemingly eternal opposition, for by very definition, east and west are irreconcilable. At the intercontinental level, the North/South gap widens as year by year the rich of the North (both East and West) become richer and the poor of the South (both East and West) become poorer. Although the terms east and west and north and south are used here to distinguish between the haves and have nots of this world, increasingly the terms become less accurate as the new industrial nations take their place in the world scene, but the division that the terms represent become more acute.

In Britain divisions increase. Urban and the suburban areas stand out in marked contrast to the decay and disintegration of the inner cities. Increasing polarisation characterises the political parties, while within families the frightening and bewildering increase in marital breakdown illustrates the effects of division at the interpersonal level.

We all bear the wounds of living in such a world. Many of us know people who, unable to bear the pain of a divided world or a divided self, will take their own lives. We, though not contemplating suicide, often must feel that life is getting out of control. To regain control of your life and time it is necessary for you to understand what it is that makes you feel torn apart and in turmoil.

In the previous round you began to work out targets for your life. Producing your list of targets was not easy. You were forced to choose, to select from all the possibilities, those dreams which were and are important to you; to ask yourself: What should I put first? How can I balance this against that? How can I integrate these two conflicting demands? As you were making your choices and deciding on your answers, you would have experienced a form of division, or conflict, within yourself. To manage your time effectively, you need to be able to face these conflicts, whatever their source.

Other People's Expectations

Other people can also cause us conflict and strain, and this is the area I want you to focus on now. Expectations place demands on your time. When too much is expected you feel forced to make choices that may bring with them feelings of guilt; for you cannot meet all that others would demand from you. Is too much expected? Such demands are a significant part of your world. Your parents may expect you to visit them weekly with the children. Your boss may expect you to work overtime. Your aunt may expect a letter once a month. And your coach expects you to use the table opposite to list all those groups of people and individuals who expect things of you. Do that now!

Let me illustrate the importance of identifying people's expectations. I was working with an international company when a senior manager asked me out for lunch. During the pleasant meal, we considered the state of the business, some staffing issues and the details of a forthcoming conference, but I sensed that there was another issue on his mind. His career took him overseas quite often and he had his children educated at boarding schools. 'How is the family?' I asked. 'Fine' he replied, and then launched into a long explanation as to why they were not as fine as he would have liked them to be!

Speaking of his oldest son, who was now seventeen and very, very different temperamentally (he confessed) from his dad, 'I just cannot reach him. I love him but he won't return my love.'

As he continued to talk, I saw clearly that the boy was destructive and aggressive, causing problems for the whole family, and that his father's strategy amounted to this: 'Perhaps if I give him his own way he will learn to love me.' This strategy was not working.

I asked him what he expected of his son and he replied without hesitation, 'I expect all my children to love me.'

'And what does your son expect of you?' I countered. The expression on his face showed that he had never ever thought of such a question! After we had talked for a long time, he came to see that he could not expect love from his son; that love is a gift

Other People's Expectations of Me	
People	**What They Expect of Me**
Family 1. Spouse	
2. Children	
3. Parents	
4. Relations	
Work 5. Boss	
6. Colleagues	
7. Subordinates	
Church and Social 8. Minister/ President	
9. Team Members	
10. Officials	
Neighbours & **Friends** 11.	
12.	
13.	
Others 14.	
15.	
16.	

not a right. Over the remains of our lunch he devised some new expectations. First, he expected his son to obey him and abide by the rules of the family — or else go his own way. That was the most that my client could expect now that his son was a young adult; and it was something he needed to achieve for the stability and health of the whole family.

Those people who are important in your life — spouse, boss, children, parents, friends will have a number of expectations of you. Have you put them down? One person I know listed over fifty expectations! Your list may not be very long, but it may well show you why you feel under pressure — if you do!

Look at your list of Other People's Expectations of Me (page 57) and ask yourself whether what is being expected of you is realistic or not. Mark with a cross those expectations that you would like to change.

The remaining time of the round will take you about 40 minutes to complete. If you do not have that amount of time, you should go on to Round Ten, then come back to this point when you can dedicate 40 minutes to establishing your priorities. Round Ten, by the way, describes how to make more time to do the things you need to do now.

So far in this round we have thought about the expectations that people have of you; about their priorities for your life. Many people spend their lives trying, often vainly, to satisfy other people's dreams. This may seem a good thing to do, but it isn't always. Your own needs have to be taken into account.

Your Basic Needs

The sociologist Abraham Maslow made a study of human motivation. What is important to people? What drives and inspires

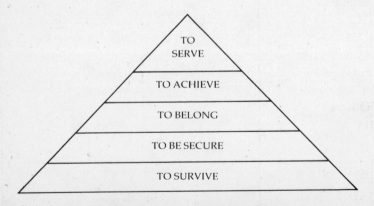

Maslow's Hierarchy of Needs

people? These questions were behind his work. Eventually he produced his now famous hierarchy of needs.[18] He said that what is important to people, what motivates people, changes from situation to situation. 'Obvious!' you say, but Maslow went on to explain that the changes were not random; they followed a pattern: a hierarchy of needs. His work has been widely developed by many writers, but the above diagram captures much of what has been written.

Survival

Maslow said, in effect, that as humans, our number one priority is to survive. This is the basis of our living, the foundation upon which our lives are built and our needs met. We need to eat, to drink and to have shelter. Faced with a life threatening situation such as being stuck in a snow drift, rather than reading a book on effective use of time, we'd be tearing it up, as fuel for a fire!

Check back to your list of targets (page 53), how many relate to survival needs? Fill in the numbers in the table below opposite 1. Survival.

My Own Life Priorities	
Maslow's Triangle	My Targets
1. Survival	
2. Security	
3. Belonging	
4. Achieving	
5. Serving	

However, survival is the lowest form of existence, and you were made for higher fulfilment than that: hence Maslow's other levels.

Security

Once your immediate physical need for survival is ensured and the book on time management is burning merrily – keeping you warm and keeping the wolves at bay – your next priority is your security. Soon the fire will go out so what you need is a stock of *Fighting for Time* to keep the fire going! We spend some eight to ten hours a day on survival and another eight to ten on achieving security – maintaining our standard of living, keeping the home together, preparing for our pension, holidays, new car, house or outfit.

With about 18 hours of the day gone that leaves relatively little time for the higher level priorities. They are called higher level since they deal with the higher aspects of our being: they deal with the quality of our life rather than its quantity. Check again your list of targets. How many relate to security needs? Fill in the number in the table above, My Own Life Priorities, opposite *2. Security*.

Belonging

So once the stack of time management books is large enough to burn all night your next priority is company. You need people to share in the warmth of the fire and perhaps read a few chapters with you; people to laugh or share your hopes and fears with. Maslow describes this priority as the need to belong – to be part of a group. In our busy days and nights this is often a neglected area – we are too preoccupied with our security. Those of us who work at a distance from home, have to leave early often before the family group is up; then arrive home tired, after all the children are in bed. Such a life leaves little time for going to the club, church or 'local' to mingle with others. On average, modern living gives little more than one hour a day for our social priorities – for our need to belong. Once again check your targets and enter the number that relate to the need to belong in the table above.

Achieving

So back to our fire, around which now sits a familiar group. Night after night you meet but now another priority makes itself known. Humans have a need for progress, for achievement. You may want to make a bigger and better fire, or invite more people to join your group or improve your reading speed!

Check your targets for achievement orientation and enter the number in the table, opposite *4. Achieving*. Be careful because there is a sense in which *every* target is an achievement statement. The key difference is that achievement relates to areas in which we are doing well but wanting to do better.

Serving

The highest level of priority, according to Maslow, is to serve. Having fulfilled your achievement needs, you can turn your attention to the needs of others. Out of your own fullness you can give to others: help them build fires, make new friends or find new books to burn! Service, according to Maslow, is the highest form of living.

It is true to say that the values of modern society have robbed most of us of our chance to find real and lasting fulfilment in life. The values of serving others, giving to and supporting those around us, for example, are all but lost to today's generations.

How much time do you have for service to others during your day? Fill in the number of your targets which relate to serving others, opposite 5. *Serving*.

What then does Maslow's table say about your life? Have a look at the numbers you have filled in.

If you have translated your dreams into a large number of survival-type targets, this would indicate that action is needed urgently and that you should begin today to achieve your targets. Round Six — Organising Your Approach, will be of special help to you.

If you have a large number of security type targets, your emphasis will need to be on longer-term issues. Round Five, which deals in detail with planning, will be helpful to you in relation to that.

Belonging-type targets indicate the need to develop your relationships and this area is dealt with in Round Ten.

Achievement-targets reflect a search for success and perfection in your life. Essential to targets of this nature are the skills of reviewing and learning from your experience. You will find Rounds Eight and Nine particularly useful in your battle to achieve these targets.

Finally, service: targets in this area indicate a degree of maturity and responsibility which is a delight for coaches to come across. To those who have a high number of targets in this area, may I say that the world needs more people like you and it needs you to be as effective as possible — so stay with it. But a word of caution: if you had a high score in the Pre-fight Check List (page 15), it may be that you have a lot of work to do before your service targets can be achieved. If you had a low number of service-type targets, don't be discouraged. You will find your

62

targets moving up Maslow's hierarchy as you become more effective in the basic areas of living.

Your Basic Priority Areas

It's time to think about your priorities. Priorities imply choice. You have priorities because you have chosen to focus on those targets which are more important to you than are others. Often the choice will be difficult — between self and the family, or between the family and work, for example. But we shouldn't avoid it for that reason.

You have already established your life vision and dreams in Round Two and your targets in Round Three. These must now be translated into priorities in all of your life's major areas — which are:

1. Your family
1a Your marriage
2. Your work (at home or away)
3. Your church or social life
4. Your leisure
5. Your neighbours
6. Yourself

Let's now examine the major life areas from which priorities may be chosen.

Your Family

Family life is under pressure. The alarming increase in divorce rates indicates that families are no longer the stable groups that we have been taught to expect. It has been estimated that for every one family which suffers divorce, another three are experiencing significant stress. If you want to keep your family together, the odds are against your success; therefore you need to work at maintaining and developing your family life. The best way to succeed is to set yourself clear targets which embrace your family needs. Look at your target statements (on page 53). Are they clear and relevant?

Your Marriage

Your relationship with your spouse can be the most precious of your human relationships. If you want to keep or make it precious, you need to work at it. Once again, check your targets. Are they significant in view of this unique relationship?

Your Work

Very often you will find that your job comes with a ready made set of targets, or objectives. These are usually produced by the employer, sometimes in conjunction with the employee. If your job is without targets then you should pay particular attention to this area. But even if your targets are set for you, you should also set your own, particularly in terms of your personal growth and development. Your work may not offer the opportunity for promotion but it will always offer the opportunity for self development.

Your Church or Social Life

The demands of modern living seem to be polarising our society. On the one hand, increasing unemployment and shorter working hours provide the opportunity for people to spend more time together. On the other hand, cuts in local government spending and the decline in the number of churches are reducing the opportunity for people to meet and socialise. What targets have you for your social and spiritual development?

Your Leisure

How do you want to use your free time? What would you like to achieve in your hobbies and pastimes? Whatever your recreation, targets will enhance your pleasure and enjoyment. Often people find that leisure time − if shared with their children or spouse, for example − can be used to meet more than one need. I do not have a separate category for leisure − I do not regard time as 'free' or spare, for me all time is real time, and so pastimes and hobbies are shared with family and friends.

Your Neighbours

We live in and benefit from our communities, but so often all that we give back are our rates and taxes. Your neighbours can represent targets for the achievement of your serving needs.

Yourself

Do not lose sight of the fact that this book is about you and for you. Setting targets for your own development is vital. Some would view it as selfish. This is a very shallow view. The great Christian commandments are to love God, and love your neighbour as yourself. How can you value your neighbours and work for their well-being if you do not value yourself and work for your own well-being?

You cannot be a whole person or achieve your life's vision without dealing with all six areas. This won't be easy because expectations and targets may clash at times. Let's see whether yours clash.

Go back to the table of Other People's Expectations of Me (page 57). Check your list against your life targets (page 53). Are there any expectations which will not be met if you pursue your new list of life targets? If all the expectations will be met, then congratulations! But what if some expectations are not going to be met?

Now you have another choice to make. Consider each expectation other people have of you which will not be met if you pursue your targets. Ask yourself this question: 'Do I want to meet this person's expectation of me?' If the answer is 'Yes' then set yourself an additional target in the appropriate life area; or try to incorporate the expectations into one of your existing targets.

If the answer is, 'No, I do not want to meet this person's expectation of me', then set yourself the targets of:

1. Communicating your decision or views.
2. Agreeing with that person a new set of expectations.

I recall a very mundane illustration of a clash of expectations. A wife expected the husband to help clear up after the evening meal, while he expected her to leave the house chores and spend the evenings relaxing with him. By the time the problem came to my attention, the conflict had escalated to such an extent that both had lost sight of the origin of it. A careful and somewhat painful unravelling of the issues began. Eventually the expectations list revealed the facts. After these had been written down and examined, both partners were able to revise their expectations and to reach a new relationship based on agreed targets − one of which was to save up for a dishwasher!

Establishing Priority Targets

A priority is some task or target which you will put before another task or target. It is something you will do, rather than doing something else, because it's more important or urgent.

Imagine that you are out shopping last thing on Saturday night. You find you have forgotten your cheque card and only have £12 in cash, you had planned to buy the week's groceries, but instead you buy only essentials − the priority items. Many different circumstances can cause us to ask questions about priorities, such as: If I can only buy a quarter of my groceries, what will make up that quarter? Or: if I can only do five of the ten jobs in the garden today, which five will it be?

So — if you could only pursue one dream, which dream would it be?

Take your list of targets from (page 53). You should have at least 18 — or at least 21 if you are married. Now select from that list the four targets which are of greatest importance to you and mark these with a P1. Now consider the remaining targets. Of those, which three are of greatest importance to you? Mark these P2.

Life Area	Priority	Target
	P1.1	
	P1.2	
	P1.3	
	P1.4	
	P2.1	
	P2.2	
	P2.3	

You have now identified the seven most important targets of your life. These are to be your new priorities. All the remaining targets will be Q's since they must wait their turn. Look back to Round One at how you spend your time, (page 34). Most people find that the way they have been spending their time bears little resemblance to their priorities. They spend their lives either on other people's priorities or on their own Q's!

Q's are often easy targets to achieve. Check whether your Q's are, generally speaking, more quickly and easily achieved than your P1's. See what I mean? The temptation is to spend your time on Q's because they are easier. But they are your secondary targets and should be given second place in your life.

Now look at your P1's. Which is the most important? Call it your P1.1 target. Rank you other P1's and P2's in the same way, ie, P1.2, P1.3, P2,1, P2.2, etc.

You have now completed Round Four. You may retire to your corner for a well-earned rest. I recommend that you have a good break at this point. Stand up if you can, have a walk around, put the book aside for an hour or for the day. There are no exercises here, so relax. In the next round we will look at strategies and planning: words which should convey the idea of getting ready for action. See you after the interval!

Round Five
Planning Your Strategy

Welcome back. You have established your vision, your dreams, your targets and your priorities. Now what do you do? The answer is: 'Plan!'

You should not be put off by the word. You do have the time and the skill to put plans together.

What do you do when you find yourself in a strange town and need to locate a street or building? You plan. We are all familiar with A-Z street guides. If you know where you want to go, the guide will show you in which area the target lies. If you know where you are and where you want to be, then the street plan allows you to plan your route.

There are some major differences between the plans that you need for effective living and the good old A-Z approach. Firstly, your targets are likely to be less definable than a street location. Secondly an A-Z presents you with a multitude of possible routes, whereas although there are many ways forward for your life, it is unlikely that you will wish or be able to plan for a whole range of possibilities. Thirdly, although towns and roads are changing rapidly, it is unlikely that the street or building will move, whereas your own targets can shift quite dramatically from month to month, or year to year. It is these differences which put people off planning. 'Why waste time planning when everything keeps changing?' I am often asked. The fact is that although planning can't stop things changing, it does help you manage change.

Planning as Preparation for Action
What do I mean by planning? Planning is preparing for action.

In order to prepare for action you need to know five things:

1. Where you want to be
2. Where you are
3. What forces are working for you
4. What forces are against you
5. How you might get there

Let's assume you're planning a trip to East Germany. You know 1 and 2 but 5 gives you a number of choices. Do you go by air, car, bus, train, ferry or barge? Your decision will be influenced by 3 and 4 — you have a passport and a visa (3) but your funds are limited and your companion does not like flying (4). Once you have decided to go by car, there is more planning to do: routes to be decided; tickets to be bought; accommodation to be booked. We can illustrate planning at its simplest like this:

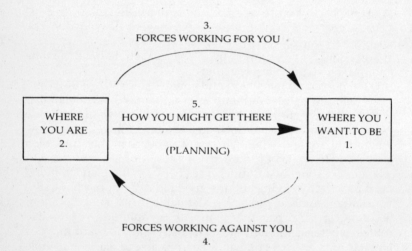

Planning can be for something as simple as a shopping list or as complex as open heart surgery. If you wish to be really effective in your life you must learn to plan effectively. As the diagram shows, this need not be too difficult a task — if we have the right attitudes.

How Do You Rate as a Planner?
The following assessment table will help you identify your attitudes and approaches to planning.

Rate Yourself as A Planner

Place a tick in the column which best describes how you feel about each statement

Statement	Strongly Agree	Agree	Disagree	Strongly Disagree	Do Not Know
1. Life is too unpredictable for planning to be of much help					
2. A daily plan for your activities, is helpful					
3. Plans are only useful if they cover all the things that can possibly go wrong.					
4. I think life should be lived and enjoyed rather than planned.					
5. Life should be taken as it comes.					
6. Planning is only useful if you have a clear idea of what you want.					
7. Plans are like rules — you should adhere to them.					
8. I believe in taking advantage of every opportunity to move my plans forward.					
9. Detailed planning restricts flexibility.					
10. My life is made up of following other people's plans					
11. Once set, plans should not be changed.					
12. Plans take the risk out of living.					

Now take your answers and place a circle around the appropriate number in the score table below. Then transfer your score to the 'My Score' column.

| Statement | SCORE | | | | | My Score |
	Strongly Agree	Agree	Disagree	Strongly Disagree	Do Not Know	
1	1	2	3	4	0	
2	4	3	2	1	0	
3	1	2	3	4	0	
4	1	2	3	4	0	
5	1	2	3	4	0	
6	4	3	2	1	0	
7	1	2	3	4	0	
8	4	3	2	1	0	
9	1	2	3	4	0	
10	1	2	3	4	0	
11	1	2	3	4	0	
12	1	2	3	4	0	
					TOTAL	

How Do You Rate?

If you scored 36 or over, planning is no problem for you. (You should check this score against your score in the Pre-fight Check List in the introduction, page 15.)

Scores between 24 and 36 indicate that you are aware of the need for planning but that its value to you is not nearly as great as it might be.

Below 24 your world is likely to be somewhat confused and perplexing. Planning does not work for you. It is perhaps worth saying that some people who are strongly religious may have a low score in this test. This may be due to their view of the world and perhaps also the view that planning is a denial of faith. If you hold this view, Round Thirteen may help you to gain more from planning.

Different Approaches to Planning

Even if your overall score may be less than satisfactory, your own particular approach to preparing for action may work well, or one of the many approaches to planning could suit you particularly well. What are the different approaches to planning?

There are five main approaches to planning:-

1. The opportunistic approach
2. The scientific approach
3. The low risk approach
4. The high risk approach, and
5. The organic approach

Let's examine each approach before you get down to the task of preparing your own plans.

The Opportunistic Approach

Most of the sea coasts of Western Europe have played host to the Viking longships at one time or another. To this day the

**For the Viking Life was Great Fun —
But Highly Uncertain**

Northern Isles of the UK have the remains of fortifications built to protect the islands from the regular visits of the blonde invaders. Place names, family names, traditions and languages are rich in the heritage brought from the northlands.

The Viking approach to planning was basically simple. There were two main points in the year — the coming of the ice and the coming of spring. With the former, the Viking longships had to be safely returned and beached. Throughout the long winter night the Norsemen would enjoy their spoils and heal the wounds from their summer expeditions. With the spring came new opportunities. The men would load the ships, honour the gods, toast one another and set off. 'Go west Norsemen!' was the cry — and they did: West to the Faroes, and Iceland; west to Greenland and — so some early maps and archaeological evidence suggest — to the North American continent.

Planning did not feature much in the Vikings' way of life. They saw life as an opportunity for adventure. Consequently, life could be fun, but was often dangerous, and usually short.

Look again at your scores in the planning questionnaire. Add your scores for questions 1, 4 and 5. If you have a total score for these three questions of six or less then you are planning your life in the manner of the Vikings. You are opportunistic. You need to have plenty of energy and flexibility, and your life is likely to be:

- unpredictable
- full of surprises and disappointments
- full of change
- full of ups and downs, peaks and troughs
- full of risk

That may be what you want; on the other hand opportunism can be disappointing.

The Scientific Approach

Few transAtlantic voyages today will occur without a very different style of planning from that used by Viking seamen. Pilot support, weather forecasts, traffic in shipping lanes, fuel supply points, ports of call, in addition to the requirements of the passengers for food, drink, linen, entertainment and medical support, all have to be considered in the planning of the voyage.

Everything Was Planned For
Except What Actually Happened

During the post-war period, companies, countries and individuals were reintroduced to the delights of scientific planning. The communist countries developed their famous five year plans while the industrial countries of the West learned to forecast the future by drawing lines forward on a graph based on what had happened in the past!

The scientific approach requires you to take account of all that you know will happen — and (sometimes) of all that you think could happen too!. During the Apollo moon shot programme, when our race was boldly going where no man had gone before, a group of scientists was appointed to identify all the things that could possibly go wrong. This was scientific planning carried to its limits.

A major problem for the scientific planner is that the degree and complexity of effort involved, makes flexibility very hard to achieve. Scientific planners, having worked so hard and juggled

74

with so many factors, are reluctant to change their plans once made. In the first world war millions of men on both sides died because the generals were committed to plans, even when it became obvious that they should have abandoned them.

Add up your scores from statement 3, 9 and 11 (page 70). If you scored less than 8 on these three questions then your life may well be characterised by the following:

- inflexibility and a tendency to keep right on to the (bitter) end of the road.
- indecision and a low level of achievement (too much analysis leading to paralysis)
- high levels of disappointment and frustration in your progress towards your targets.
- too much time spent on thinking and not enough time left for action.

One classic example of the limitations of scientific planning was the Titanic disaster. The last word in technology, fully equipped for comfort and efficiency, she nevertheless sank. Those in charge were so committed to their belief that the Titanic was unsinkable, that they didn't respond flexibly to the actual situation until it was too late. Similarly, however 'scientific' and thorough our planning is, we have to allow for the possibility of something unexpected happening which might involve us in scrapping all our plans and doing something completely different!

Exhaustive planning may seem to take the uncertainty out of the future but more often than not reduces your capacity to change.

The Low Risk Approach

The longships and the Titanic provided examples of opportunistic and/or scientific approaches; a third approach – the low risk approach – could be likened to what the Polaris submarine does: it keeps its head down and its sights low and only surfaces when there's no danger! Those who plan their lives in this way often miss out on joy and a sense of achievement. The low risk planners set their targets low and are often too influenced by the opinions and actions of others to live their lives to anything like the full.

If you scored less than 8 on questions 7, 10 and 12 then you probably plan your life in this low risk way: constantly looking over your shoulder, as it were, to see who might be attempting to get in your way, or for fear of criticism, preferring to follow

**Like the Polaris Submarine
Some People Surface Only When It's Safe**

other people's plans for you rather than planning a life of your own.

A major problem for low risk planners is that eventually, like the submarine, they must surface for air. They must declare their position sooner or later, and, as the U-boats of the last war proved, there is nothing more vulnerable than a submarine on the surface!

The High Risk Approach

The *Navigatio* manuscript, written around the tenth century, gives an account of the first Atlantic crossing by St Brendan, the sixth century Irish monk, in a coracle, or curragh — a fragile craft of oxen skin and timber frame.

In 1976 the internationally known voyager, Tim Severin embarked on a repeat voyage to prove the possibility of what seemed to be simply folklore. He built a boat as nearly as possible to sixth century design. The early part of Severin's journey took the craft up the west coast of Ireland and across to the Hebrides off the Scottish west coast where one member of the crew had to be put ashore due to injury. A new member was

High Risk Planners – Don't Plan

needed. They found one – a high risk planner – on the island of Iona.

In Severin's own words:

> I was accosted on the beach by a fantastic figure.
> 'I say,' he began excitedly, 'Are you the skipper of that strange looking boat? I must say, it's fascinating. I'm told you're looking for a crew member.'
> 'Yes,' I answered cautiously ...
> 'I'm the captain of that blue yacht out there. We do charters through the Hebrides. But I'd like to join your crew, if you'll have me ... I've got two brothers. They can take over for the summer.' Then as an afterthought, he asked, 'By the way, where are you going in that boat?'

Severin comments, 'He was one of nature's leap-before-you-look characters whose bravado carried him head over heels through life.'[19]

And so it was, after nearly two months at sea the Brendan

voyage was proved feasible and a young west coast charter yacht captain who did not know where he was going arrived there.

High risk planners – don't! They choose not to plan, which is a plan in itself. Nine out of ten people are high risk planners because they plan not to plan.

The Organic Approach

We read a lot about organic activities these days. There are organic gardening methods, cosmetics and medicines. The word organic in these contexts conveys the idea of naturalness – the opposite of artificial or forced growth. So organic planning is natural, unforced, unartificial.

Such planning takes account of:

1. Your targets
2. Your present situation
3. Your strengths and your supporters
4. Your weakness and your opposition
5. Your next steps.

Let's examine each aspect of organic planning.

Your targets

Look again at your targets (page 53). Are they unique? Are they the targets that only you could achieve, or are they targets that anyone could have? If they are so general that they could belong to anyone, then rewrite them to make them uniquely yours. For example, if you have written 'my wife, 'my husband' or 'my children', put in their names instead.

Your present situation

Where are you now in relation to your targets? Complete this sentence in five different ways for your P1.1 target (See page 65).

In relation to this target, my present situation is:

1. _____
2. _____
3. _____
4. _____
5. _____

It is important to be realistic about your present situation. If you think that you might not be honest with yourself, then check what you write with someone who knows you well.

When planning your strategy for meeting your targets, you will need to be clear about your current situation — for that is your starting point.

Your strengths and supporters

What is working in your favour? What strengths have you and on whom can you rely for support? For your P1.1 target complete the following sentences in three different ways:

In relation to my P1.1 target my personal strengths are:

1._____

2._____

3._____

I can look for support from:

4._____

5._____

6._____

Your weaknesses and opposition

What and who is working against you? We are all flawed beings, and we must never forget this. Much disappointment and depression arises from overly high expectations of ourselves, either because we are not assessing ourselves realistically or because we haven't taken account of what we are up against.

Complete the following sentence for your P1.1 target:

In relation to this my P1.1 target my weaknesses are:

1._____

2._____

3._____

I have to contend with:

4._____

5._____

6._____

Your next steps

Part of planning is preparation for action and involves taking account of your strengths and weaknesses, so that you can identify the next steps.

The table which follows may help you to do this. In column seven state your P1.1 target; in column one, your present situ-

(1) My Present Situation	(2) My Strengths	(3) My Weaknesses	(4) My Next Possible Steps	(5) The Time Required	(6) Review Date and Method	(7) My Target

An Organic Planning Chart

Columbus Made the Best Use of His Resources

ation; in column two, your strengths; in column three your weaknesses. Then in column four set down your next possible steps, and in column five state how long it will take to achieve each step. Be realistic! In column six write the date on which you will review progress, and the method you will use. Now do this for your P1.2 target. (See page 65.)

The organic approach to planning is best characterised by Christopher Columbus on his westward voyage to the East Indies. With a vision and a small fleet he sailed west towards what most people thought of as the edge of the world.

But Columbus made the best use of his resources, the most of his strengths, minimised his weaknesses and overcame the barriers to his success. How did he operate?

(1) He had a clear vision of where he wanted to go.

(2) He made the best use of his resources. Although his crew were rebellious, fearful and sick, he managed to use them to the best of their capabilities.

(3) He made the best use of the currents and winds that he encountered in moving his fleet further west every day.

(4) He made the most of his land fall — not the East Indies, but America!

His belief in himself and his crew brought prosperity to his nation and changed the course of the world's history. You could also change the world — by changing yourself. Organic planning will help you.

The chart (page 79) is a powerful tool for the planning of your priority targets. It should be completed for each of your targets. Use one planning sheet per target.

It is recommended that you write out only one planning chart per week. Heavyweight learners may wish to finish more quickly, but see the exercise at the end of this round.

A very useful tip is to complete each planning chart without putting anything in column four. Then take your unfinished planning chart and share it with a friend. Ask your friend to suggest possible steps for column four. This helps to generate alternative ways forward. When you have completed column four, reorder the steps chronologically and set times against them. You now have a simple planning tool which you can use — and you have come successfully through Round Five.

The interval training exercise overleaf is designed to ensure that you apply the lessons of this round effectively. So complete the exercises now before you have a break.

Interval Training Exercise – All Learning Weights
Complete the following planning chart:

My Present Situation	I have carried out a trial exercise on only my P1.1 target
My Strengths	
My Weaknesses	
My Next Possible Steps	
The Time Required	
My Target	To prepare a planning chart for all P1 & P2 targets within 8 weeks
My Review: Dates/Method	Share my Chart with a friend every Friday for the next 8 weeks

Round Six

Organising Your Resources

Build today, then, strong and sure,
With a firm and ample base;
And ascending and secure
Shall tomorrow find its place.[20]

I was once asked to serve on a committee in a small church in a rural area. The church building and grounds were not impressive. Paint was flaking off the walls, weeds were rampant and there was a general air of neglect. I was given the Minute Book 'for background reading', as the chairman put it. It recorded a history of disorganisation. At each of the annual church meetings for the previous four years a decision had been taken to refurbish the church but nothing had happened. The paint continued to flake, the weeds to grow. Money was not the problem; manpower, although limited, was available. They knew what they wanted to do but they never got around to it. They were not organised.

Planning a Year's Targets

How many times do you know what you want to do but you never seem to find the time to do it?

Having fought your way to Round Six the last thing you should want to do is retire with a fist full of unaccomplished targets and priorities. So let me teach you how to organise yourself. The first tool that you need is a simple year planner for your targets. Many diaries are now incorporating year planners but you can easily make one. Use the example overleaf as a model.

Annual Target Planner			19
Week	Week	Week	Week
1	14	27	40
2	15	28	41
3	16	29	42
4	17	30	43
5	18	31	44
6	19	32	45
7	20	33	46
8	21	34	47
9	22	35	48
10	23	36	49
11	24	37	50
12	25	38	51
13	26	39	52
This Year's Targets In Priority Order			

P1.1 (eg) Reduce my weight by 5 kilos by June 30 (Week 26)
P1.2 (eg) Give up smoking for 3 months starting July 28
   (Week 30)
P1.3 (eg) Paint the outside of house by end October (Week 43)
P1.4 etc
P2.1
P2.2
P2.3
etc

Your priority targets, your Ps, should be listed in the lower half of your planner (three examples are given). Now transfer your priority codes (eg P1.1, P1.2, P1.3 etc) to the upper part of the planner prefixing each with the letter 'S' for start and 'F' for finish. Thus P1.1 might begin on the fourteenth week and finish at the end of the twenty-sixth week. Organise all your targets in this way. This will ensure a starting and finishing date for all your priorities. Getting organised is about how you plan your moments, so let's coin a new proverb 'Take care of your moments and your months will take care of themselves.' Although, as you have learned, the months only take care of themselves if you have set your targets clearly. Nevertheless, once the targets have been set and once you have planned your priorities on your annual planner, then next you need a daily planner.

A daily planner should be as simple as you can make it. The easiest daily planner is an action list. An action list is just a list of your day's priorities.

Get yourself a small pad or note book. One about 6 inches by 4 inches (15cm x 10cm) will do, preferably with its own pencil/pen attached.

Keep the pad by your bedside. As you retire each night jot down your priorities for the next day. As you rise, check your list and add to it if necessary those priorities that you omitted or overlooked the evening before.

Tear off your action list from the pad and carry it with you throughout the day. Score off each action as it is completed, add new actions as they come to mind during the day. Your daily planner is a real working tool. By the end of the day you will be encouraged by how many priorities have been achieved. A more detailed planner is shown below.

Daily Planning

Date _____ Month _____ 19 _____   _____DAY

Appointments	Urgent/Actions	Projects	Others
7:			
8:			
9:			
10:			
11:			
12:			
1:			
2:	'Phone	Letters	Secretary
3:			
4:			
5:			
6:			
7:			
8:			
9:			
10:			

Making the Best Use of Time

The point of this yearly and daily planning is so that you can make the best use of your time. Here are some suggestions. Schedule your regular activities — answering mail, making telephone calls, cleaning rooms, for example — for the same time each day. A routine helps with routine tasks. It is very unlikely that you will always be able to do your routine tasks at exactly the same time but having a schedule like this will help you to keep tabs on what still needs to be done.

The Telephone

Telephone calls are time thieves. Plan your outgoing calls. Ring between 8.30 and 9.20 am if you want to catch people at their desks. Time is often wasted on calls·to people who are not in. Use an egg timer by the telephone to help you time your calls.

If you are busy when you receive a call, let the caller know what you are doing and that it is important 'Nice of you to call Mary. I am right in the middle of baking/writing/planning etc. Can you call me back this afternoon?'

John Humble an international management consultant cites telephone interruptions as one of the greatest time problems for managers. The other major problems are —

Meetings — too many, too long and badly run.
Unexpected visitors — people dropping in.
Poor delegation — doing what others could do just as well.[21]

So — how can you deal better with meetings, paper work and visitors? How can you delegate better?

Meetings

I remember talking to a manager who had recently been appointed and had inherited a meeting overload.

'Just look at my diary!' he complained to me. 'More than three days a week in meetings!' 'What do you suggest?'

I replied, 'Begin by cancelling one meeting in three and reducing the time of the remainder by half. He said, 'But I don't know which ones are important.' My reply was: 'True. But your secretary will know.'

He lifted the phone and called her in. Then he said, 'Jean, I want one meeting in three cancelled — you'll know which — and every other meeting has to have its time cut by half.'

The effects of his decision were soon felt across the whole

organisation as other managers took his lead, meetings were cancelled, paper work was reduced and time was made available for the real work.

The rule is: when you think you need a meeting — think again! Ask yourself in relation to every meeting —

1. What is the purpose? If you cannot think of a worthwhile one, cancel the meeting or send your apologies.
2. Who needs to attend? If the answer is, 'Not me' then don't go.
If there are people coming who have nothing to contribute, ask them to do something else rather than attend.
3. Could the meeting be shorter? If so, shorten it.
4. Could regular meetings be held less frequently? If so then cut the frequency by half — to start with.
5. What can I do to make better use of the time in the meeting? Anything? Then do it.

Running meetings

When a meeting is unavoidable, keep to these rules.

1. Inform people well in advance of the purpose, time, place and duration of the meeting.
2. Give as much information, pre-reading and preparation time as possible.
3. Produce an agenda well in advance.
4. Start on time — do not wait for the late comers. Even if you are the only one there on time, as chairman, begin!
5. The first item on the agenda should be the identification of Any Other Business. Ask members to state, at the outset, if they have any other items to be dealt with. This ensures that you are not left with major items of surprise business to deal with in five minutes at the close of the meeting!
6. Divide your agenda into two sections:
     (i) Standing items ie. those items which always appear — apologies, minutes of last meeting, matters arising, finance, fabric, etc.
     (ii) Special topics. Never hold a team meeting without at least one special topic (See 8 overleaf).

7. Put a target against every item on the agenda and add a time limit. Stick to your time. When the time is almost up draw attention to the time limit. When the time is up, say so. If necessary, extend the time but tell the team you are allowing more time. State the new time allocation and stick to it. If the target has not been reached at the end of the extension then you decide, or defer the decision till another meeting.

8. Special topics give the meeting interest and an opportunity for creativity and forward thinking. Avoid having more than three special topics at any one meeting.

For each special topic item state:

(i) The title of the topic
(ii) The purpose of the topic
(iii) The procedure which will be followed
(iv) Any advanced pre-reading/thinking needed
(v) The time to be allocated
(vi) The target of this discussion

9. Review each meeting. Put 'Meeting Review' on the agenda and state the target. For example, to agree one action which will improve the next meeting.

10. Finish on time.[22]

Assessing meetings

Whether or not you are the chairperson, keep your eyes and ears open for problems during the meetings. It is much better to take corrective action during a meeting than to wait until the end-of-the-meeting review. The following table will help identify what to look for.

Meeting Review

1. Was the meeting well run? YES/NO

2. How much real progress do you think the meeting made?

None
at all
|___|___|___|___|
Great
progress

3. Did the team work well together or did it tend to split up into small factions?

Split
up
|___|___|___|___|
Worked
well together

4. Was the meeting clear about its targets or was there some confusion?

Con-
fusion
|___|___|___|___|
Clear

5. Did all members of the meeting participate fully or was the meeting dominated by one or a few individuals?

Domi-
nated
|___|___|___|___|
Participative

6. How much digression from the targets of the meeting took place?

A lot of
digression
|___|___|___|___|
No
digression

7. State one action that **you** could take next time the team meets which would improve performance.

_____

_____

_____

Paperwork

When people speak of having paperwork problems they could be referring to any or all of the following:

1. Receiving the paper
2. Handling the paper
3. Responding to the paper
4. Storing the paper
5. Retrieving the paper

Let us consider some of the techniques for each.

Receiving the paper

Paperwork arrives on your desk or kitchen table via the post by hand ('Mum, there's a letter from my teacher. Can I have a biscuit? Yeah, I dropped it in a puddle. Sorry.')

In households with canine members, post may arrive slightly wet and chewed!

The first thing to say about paper work is, 'Deal with it when it suits you.' You need not open letters as soon as they arrive. Deal with them at the best time for you. Most people respond to letters just as they do to the telephone — dropping everything to deal with it immediately. Do not be driven by other people's priorities. Open the post when you plan to and not when it arrives — as an interruption — on your door mat.

Secondly have a place for unopened letters. Call it an 'in tray' if you like, just as long as you know where to find them. Make sure everyone in the office or home knows where to put any post which arrives.

Thirdly do not open the post until you are ready to deal with it. You waste time reading it twice.

Fourthly, if you receive large batches of post on a regular basis, try to schedule your time accordingly. Better still try to arrange for the post to arrive when it best suits you.

Handling the paper

The golden rule is 'Handle each piece of paper only once.' This means not opening mail until you can deal with it, so set aside time for it when you are ready.

The first step is to classify your mail in some way. One useful approach is to use a four category classification called AIRS. In this method all paperwork is put into one of the following categories:

A – Action
I – Information
R – Reading
S – Scrap

The post brings things which you would do well to *scrap*. Probably a quarter of your post is junk mail. 'If you reply immediate-
ly/today/without delay/at once/within ten days, you will receive
a gift/prize/entry for a grand draw/holiday for two/a million
pounds – or more unwanted mail next month!' Don't even
bother opening this type of post. Scrap it.

Plenty of *reading* matter comes in the post. Long letters, circu-
lars, magazines and the like take a long time to read. Do not
read them when they arrive unless you have planned to do so.
Instead put them in a reading file. Reading can be fitted in to
those spare moments in between larger tasks, or carried out on
buses, cars, trains and planes, or over a cup of coffee. Most of
my writing and all of my reading is done while I am travelling.
Do not use prime time for reading things which come in the
post; this sort of reading is rarely a P1 or even a P2. Make your
reading a Q, but try to set aside time to clear your reading file
once a week.

Much *information* comes via the postman. Some of this must
be read on the day that you receive it: material for a meeting that
day or information you've been waiting for, for example. Once
again, choose the time during the day that suits you best, not
necessarily the moment the post arrives. At a coffee break,
perhaps, you can relax, refresh yourself and catch up on your
information – three tasks at once!

Responding

Some of the mail calls for *action*; it requires a response from
you. You may wish to reply immediately or within a week.
Again keep an action file and clear it daily. Progress all the items
in it on a daily basis. But once more let me stress – do it when it
best suits you! Remember it is quicker to telephone than to
write.

What should you do with mail that requires action but not
immediately? Invest in an expanding file. A concertina type file
is excellent for holding action material which is 'pending.' But
you need to keep it organised. Most people use the 'heap'
system for their pending papers and then waste so much time
searching through the heap for what they need. Do not be a
paper shuffler. Your expanding file should be set up in date
order – ie, the date on which you must take the action. This

type of filing is called 'bring-up' filing, or 'brief-up' filing. It brings up your paper work when you want it. Instead of having the file pockets labelled finance, insurance, bank, income, or tax, the files are labelled January, February, March ... If you have masses of paper, you might need to put it into a weekly bring-up file; some very busy people may need a daily one.

Storing and Retrieving

Filing is not the same as storing. Filing is for material that you wish to *retrieve*; for items that you are likely to need access to. A good filing system makes its material very accessible. The ten commandments of good filing are:

1. Label all your files clearly
2. Keep a record of your file headings
3. Keep your file categories small
4. Never have a miscellaneous file
5. Clear your files at least once per year
6. Store old files; don't file them!
7. Mark key papers with a coloured marker or label
8. Keep often used files together
9. Keep key documents, certificates etc together
10. Keep your files thin — no more than 2cm thick

There is no easy way to run a filing system. It takes — but saves — time.

Visitors

So much for the paper, now what about the people? Sometimes, I wish I could file — or better store — some of them! You may not be able to file them, but you are able to organise them.

For paper, we used AIRS as a mnemonic. For people, GRACES rather than airs are required!

People drop in. They say, 'Just passing, thought I'd pop in for a cuppa,' or, 'I saw your light on and so ...' If you are lucky the visitor will only be wanting to pass a few moments, but on the other hand hours of your time could be wasted.

Faced with an unexpected visitor your first challenge is to decide whether you have a time waster on your hands or whether you have someone with a legitimate problem or need that should take priority over what you are doing. Hence you need some social graces! Deal with the visitor in an orderly manner and according to the following procedure:

> G — Greet only. Say, 'Hi,' and go back to your work.
> R — Receive. Say, 'Come in. Nice to see you,' and then go on with your work.
> A — Accompany. Say, 'Hello, glad you stopped by, so-and-so was looking for you. Let me take you along,' then get on with your work.
> C — Confer. Recognise that this is someone who needs your time as a priority and give him ten minutes.
> E — Embrace. Put on the kettle for this one is serious and urgent.
> S — See off. Make it quite clear that you are busy and cannot stop your work, but would be delighted to spend time later.

Always let the unexpected visitor know what you are doing and how important it is. If they must see you — must they see you now? Can it wait till coffee, lunch, tomorrow, next week? If so, then schedule the time with them when it best suits you.

All this may sound a bit hard, but remember you have two opponents — yourself and others. There is little to be gained by being tough on yourself while allowing others to waste the time you have gained.

Round Ten will help you if you find it difficult to say, 'No' to the time wasters. Before reading on, make a list of those people who waste your time!

Delegation

After paperwork and people comes delegation. This is something that everyone can do. It is not just an activity for managers; mothers can do it, as can teachers and ministers. One good rule is: Try to eliminate before you delegate. Before you engage on any task. Ask yourself these questions:

1. Must it be done at all?

If the answer is, 'No,' then scrap it. If the answer is, 'Yes,' then ask yourself:

2. Is this the best time to do it?

If the answer is, 'No,' then reschedule it. If the answer is, 'Yes' then ask yourself.

3. Can someone else do it?

If the answer is, 'Yes' then give it to that person to do. If the answer is, 'No,' then ask yourself what the most effective way of doing the job would be — then do it that way.

The diagram below shows how to deal with activities according to their urgency and importance.

	NOT URGENT	URGENT
IMPORTANT	3. PLAN IT	4. DO IT
NOT IMPORTANT	1. LEAVE IT	2. DELEGATE IT

1. If a task is not important and not urgent, then leave it.
2. If a task is not important but urgent, then delegate it.
3. If a task is important but not urgent, then plan when best to do it.
4. If a task is both important and urgent, then do it — now.

Ten commandments for effective delegation

Let us look for a moment longer at delegation. We need not be in an organisation in order to be able to delegate: we only need to have someone else around! Here are ten commandments for effective delegation.

1. Provide complete information on the task. What is the target? When is it to be completed? What standards are you expecting?
2. Define precisely the limits of responsibility of the person in relation to the task. Satisfy yourself that he understands them, eg How much money can be spent, what equipment can be used, to whom can he talk?

3. Don't provide the answers but help the person to find them. Where might he look for information, guidance etc?

4. Don't make the decisions for the person – give him as much freedom as you can.

5. Do not be hasty in criticising mistakes. You might not have made the same mistake, but you might have made another.

6. Follow up on delegation. Agree when you will check to see that progress is being made.

7. Encourage the initiative of the other person so that he can cope with emergencies if they arise, rather than running back to you.

8. Never publicly countermand a decision taken by the person to whom you have delegated. Allow him to reverse it.

9. Back up your people to the limit that your conscience will allow.

10. Accept responsibility for all decisions that you delegate.

Barriers to Delegation

There are many reasons why you will find delegation difficult. The table overleaf gives a few of them. See which apply to you.

I Do Not Delegate Because	Applies to me	
	Yes	No
1. No one can do it as well as I can.		
2. I cannot trust anyone.		
3. No one has the skills.		
4. It's my responsibility.		
5. It takes too long to explain.		
6. It is quicker doing it myself.		
7. I have been let down too often.		
8. I like doing it.		
9. People expect me to do everything.		
10. I have more flexibility if I do things myself.		
11. I work better on my own.		
12. No one has any spare time.		
13. No one will accept the work.		
14. I prefer to make the decisions.		
15. I like to keep control.		
16. I have no time to keep chasing people.		
17. It is more bother than it's worth.		
18. I cannot afford a mistake.		
19. *		
20. *		
TOTAL		

* I am delegating these two to you. Write your own excuses!

You will never learn to live effectively unless you are able to make use of the human resources around you. It is true that some things cannot be delegated but these should be no more than 20% of your tasks, such as reading this book!

Yes, you have actually made it through another round! You are now in the position of having:

1. A daily work plan
2. An annual target planner
3. A means of making better use of meetings
4. A paper handling code – AIRS

5. A framework for dealing with people – GRACES.
6. A guide for delegating tasks
7. A whole set of reasons for continuing to do tasks that other people would be happy to do for you!

So picking up on delegation, let us carry out an exercise to reduce the demands on your time.

Interval Training Exercises

Heavyweight exercises
Choose a number of your regular tasks or duties which in total amount to 60 minutes per week and eliminate them!

Middleweight exercises
Choose one task which you do on a weekly basis and halve the time you spend on it next week and for the next three weeks.

Lightweight exercises
Choose one activity which takes you more than 30 minutes each week and reduce the time you spend on it by 5 minutes each week for the next three weeks.

Round Seven
Using Your Experience

Many of us are less successful than we need be because we forget to learn from our successes. There is a strange fascination in picking at our sores and focusing on our failings. Instead of learning from what works for us, we build up long lists of what doesn't work!

Thinking Positively

Perhaps as you read this you are thinking to yourself: 'I'm only at page 99 and only at the beginning of Round Seven.' A more positive attitude would be to think 'I've already reached page 99 and have already, in terms of time management:

- identified my strengths and weaknesses.
- found out about my learning weight.
- surveyed my day and assessed those activites that I would like to change.
- began to establish a vision for my life.
- set targets and priorities.
- prepared plans.
- begun to organise myself

These achievements represent a great deal.

Learning from Your Highs and Lows

The early rounds are not easy in any fight, because then your opposition is strongest and your confidence lowest; so it is especially important for you to focus now on your successes. If you do this, you will inevitably have to think of your unsuccessful times, too.

Spend fifteen minutes reviewing your life and make a list on separate paper of its key events. Make sure you list the bad times as well as the good times. Start from today and work back to your earliest memories. You will find that you have fewer entries as you go further back in your life.

Now imagine that the line below represents your life to date, divided into equal portions. From your list of key events pick out the four most important good times and the four most important bad times. Transfer these eight points onto your life line, putting the good times above the line and the bad times below the line in chronological order. The higher you place a good time, the better it was, while the lower you place a bad time, the worse it was. Now draw a continuous line from birth until now which passes through your eight points.

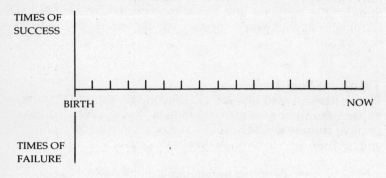

Your Life Line

Uncovering Your Pattern

Focus now on the present. Are you at a peak or trough in your life? On the crest of a wave or in the depths?

Either way, you must proceed with caution, for you will be vulnerable in the whole area of change. If you are in rough seas, you will be longing for calmer waters. But you may feel too tired or afraid to do anything about it. Or else your desperation will prompt an unwise action. If, on the other hand, you're going through a good time, you may not see any need to change even when this would be advisable.

So, whether you're high or low — take care. Proceed step by step. Learn the pace and rhythms that are right for you.

Learn from your mistakes, too. Do you do this or do you make the same mistakes again and again? Let's see if you can think about and learn from your successes now. Draw a diagram as shown below, with seven days marked out and each day divided into four spaces representing:

> Early morning
> Mid morning
> Afternoon
> Evening

Now, in the same way as you drew your life line, draw a line for last week which shows the ups and downs in the area of your life from which you chose your P1.1, eg marriage or self (see page 65).

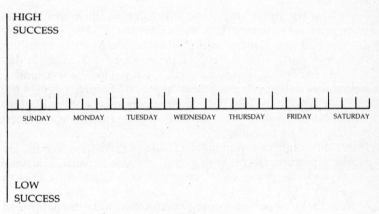

Your Week Line

Look now at your times of success. What was I doing? What was happening? Who was there? Where was I? How did I feel? You will find it helpful to write down your answers to these questions.

Now ask: What had these times of high success in common? Was it an activity? Was it a place? Was it a person? Was it a *time*?

This last question is important. Each of us works to and lives by an inner rhythm. Some of us are early birds, some late starters, some afternoon types, some late evening enthusiasts. Look again at your success line. Is there a daily pattern? Discovering our rhythm is helpful in the fight for a more effective use of time. Whether a pattern is obvious or not, one week is probably not an adequate basis for analysis. In the interval at the end of this round we shall carry out some additional exercises to help you discover the secrets of your own success.

Let us look in more detail for a moment at the times of your success. For most of us there will be a pattern to our times of success, those times when we feel able and strong will come at regular intervals for us. Likewise those times when we feel weak and unable to cope will come at predictable times.

What happens when your high energy levels coincide with times of high demands on you? The outcome is positive. You have the energy and motivation to respond and you feel in control of the situation. When the demand cycle coincides with your capacity cycle then life is indeed worth living.

What happens when you feel weary and low in confidence just when the demands are piling up? The outcome is likely to be failure.

Look at the figure opposite. This example illustrates the demand line over the four days and shows that Friday and Sunday are times of low demand while Saturday and Monday are times of high demand. This is a typical pattern for the Monday/Friday worker. On Friday things are winding down for the weekend — demand is falling off. But Friday night and Saturday brings the pressure of family life — socialising, organising the children, sitting on the parish council, running the garden fete etc. Then Sunday is more relaxing.

But although the demand has altered from the day to day working pattern, the body rhythm continues as usual. The daily cycle produces peaks of effectiveness (1,3,5,7) and troughs of low energy, (2,4,6 and 8).

Note that this person's energy peaks coincide reasonably well with the high demands of Saturday morning (3) and late Saturday afternoon (5) but in between, at the peak demand time, he is at a low point (4). The other low points (6 and 8) occur at non-critical points on the demand cycle and therefore don't matter. But what of the times when demand is low and energy high (5 and 7)? Ever been asked, 'Why can't you just sit down and relax?' If so, you'll probably know all about the frustrations of low demand and high energy; of itching to do something when there's nothing to do or others don't want you to do anything!

Working with Your Pattern

As far as this is possible, you should plan your day to suit your rhythms. Here's how to do that:

1. Listen to your inner rhythms and note when you
feel tired and when you feel strong.

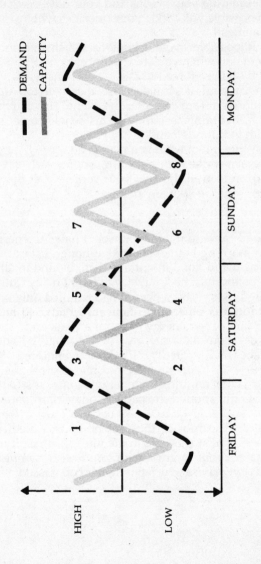

The Demand/Capacity Cycle

2. Pay attention to your successes and failures; learn to be aware of situations which are easy for you to manage and those which are difficult for you.

3. Schedule your weeks and your days so that as far as possible you tackle your priorities when you are at your best.

4. If possible avoid situations which demand a lot from you when you are at a low ebb.

5. If you are forced to tackle problems when you are not at your best make sure that you top up your batteries before and after the event. This can be done by scheduling 'a cuppa' (This whole topic is dealt with in Rounds 9 and 12.)

6. Write down what you plan to do.

7. Keep a diary for a month, noting each day when things go well. Review your successes at the end of the month to spot any patterns.

A friend came to me for counsel. 'I have no energy' she said. 'By mid morning I am exhausted although I start the day full of enthusiasm and good intentions. I am behind in all areas of my life and, although the family try to help I really cannot go on.' It transpired that visits to her GP had resulted only in the issue of drugs to improve her night-time rest. I advised her to keep an hourly diary of her energy cycle for a week and come back with the results. Four days later my 'phone rang. 'It's coffee and biscuits!' she said excitedly, 'Pardon?' I enquired. 'Coffee!' she repeated — 'It happens after my mid morning cup of coffee. Within twenty minutes my energy's gone. It's happened each day but I only spotted the pattern today!' Further data collected by her over the next two weeks began a process which changed her life. At the root of the problem was a medical condition which a specialist was able to identify. As a result of her simple attempts to come to grips with low energy symptoms she uncovered a weakness which her doctor had missed.

Interval Training Exercise

For heavyweight learners

Contrast your times of success with your times of failure both in your week and in your life. What are the essential differences between your times of success and your times of failure.

For middleweight learners

Share with someone who knows you well, both your life line and your success line for last week. Ask them if they recognise your peaks and troughs. Consider with them other times of success and failure in your life. Try to discover a pattern behind the situations in which you are generally successful.

For lightweight learners

Make a list of the important tasks that you have to do next week and prepare a plan to enable you to do those tasks, as far as possible, at the times when you are your best.

Round Eight

Reviewing Your Progress

As you enter the second half of the contest (Yes, you are half way through!) it is important that you keep your eyes firmly fixed on the targets that you have set for yourself and that you do not lose sight of the progress you have made already. Reviewing helps you to do this, and to recommit yourself to your targets, encouraged by what you have achieved so far; it also helps you overcome persistent problems.

Questions to Ask

Review is a mechanism which helps the learning process. Reviews can be long and formal like public enquiries, or brief and informal.

Whatever your approach your attitude should be positive.

Here are some good questions to ask:

1. What is working well?
2. Where are the success areas?
3. Why am I making progress?
4. What has encouraged me?
5. What strengths am I showing?

In terms of those areas in which more effort is required, once again a positive tone is helpful. Ask:

6. Where can I make more progress?
7. What opportunities still exist?
8. What more can I do?
9. What challenges remain?
10. What is working in my favour?
11. What will I do now?
12. Do my targets, priorities or plans need changing?

The focus should always be on your success, for here you can discover what you can do that works. If you focus on failure you only learn what does not work.

You should review all that you do. Every activity, every experience of life is a source of learning for you, and every lesson learned is an opportunity for improvement. You should review your plans and progress, too.

How to Review

There are a number of approaches to review. Here is one:

This simple model (which unfortunately few people actually ever bother to use) helps considerably next time round. It is like a score card in that it tells you the outcome. Did you win or did you lose? Sometimes this is referred to as the post mortem or static approach, because the review follows the action, just as a post mortem follows rather than precedes death.

Another idea is to review before the action is complete – at a half-way point, for example; just as a football team might have a half-time chat with their coach, so that they can monitor the action up to that point and take steps to improve their performance while the match is in progress. This is sometimes called a mechanistic approach and works rather like a thermostat which 'reviews' the conditions and breaks the circuit when the pre-selected temperature is reached. Though better than the static, the mechanistic approach has its limitations.

A more sophisticated approach would be to have a review system which focuses on the initial target behind the plan. In this, the dynamic system, the plan itself is changed if your review of your actions indicates that this is necessary.

Even this falls short, however, of what is needed in a world in which growth and change are all around us. In such a world you need a review process which is similarly 'alive' and organic! – a continuous review not only of actions and plans but also for your learning process, so that you know how best you learn, whether it's through doing, experimenting, watching others, reading, or whatever. This way of reviewing, the organic way, ensures that you have all the information you need and are kept aware of changes in the environment, in yourself and in those around you. In the diagram below, which shows the basic model applied to your life and time management, the word *review* is central because only if we know how we are doing, will we be able to set about doing better. Check back to the Pre-fight Check List, page 15. How well did you do on review?

When to Review

Obviously you shouldn't spend all your time reviewing; but you should allocate some time to this key activity. The following guidelines may be helpful.

1. Visions should be reviewed every three years.
2. Dreams should be reviewed each year.
3. Targets should have reviews built into them. (See page 79.) The same is true for priorities and plans.
4. Organisations should be reviewed annually.
5. Action should be being reviewed continually.
6. Learning should be reviewed annually.
7. Meetings should be reviewed at each meeting. (See page 89.)

What this means in effect is that you should set aside at least one day – preferably once a year to conduct a review of your life and progress. It is useful to consider this as a husband and wife event for those who are married.

Ideas for a Review Day

Your review day should be a special event. There are a number of ways in which its importance can be signified. For example you may go away for the day – to a public library, a cathedral or an hotel, perhaps – where you can be alone and quiet. Some people find that an overnight stay at a hotel the night before their quiet day is beneficial.

On the review day you will find it helpful to have with you:

1. Your life vision statement
2. Your list of dreams
3. Your current planning sheets for your priorities
4. Your annual priority planner
5. A diary for this year and the next year
6. Plenty of paper, pencils and rubber
7. Your copy of *Fighting for Time*

Spend the first half hour of your review day making a list of all the changes which have taken place in your life during the past year. These changes should cover, health, wealth, home, work, social and spiritual matters, etc. Give yourself the full half hour, but no more. If you finish earlier go back through your diary to refresh your memory. If you have not finished in 30 minutes then stop anyway and move on to the next activity.

Next take 30 minutes to make a list of those things that during the year you have done more of and less of. Take a sheet of paper for the 'more of's' and one for the 'less of's', and give 15 minutes only to each sheet.

You now have three pieces of paper – one with all your changes, a second with the 'more of's' and a third with the 'less of's'.

Take the next half hour to think about whether you are glad or sad about the items on your sheets. To help you here you may refer back to your vision, dreams and plans.

At the end of the half hour rate the year that has gone by overall on the scale. For a husband and wife team this is a particularly helpful exercise.

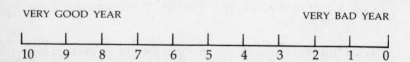

VERY GOOD YEAR									VERY BAD YEAR
10	9	8	7	6	5	4	3	2	1	0

Now you need to have a break. If possible go outside or into another room for a cup of coffee or tea. If you have chosen a library or art gallery try to find a picture that you can sit in front of while you have your refreshment. Take a break of 30 minutes.

Return to your review location and spend 15 minutes re-reading and revising your life time vision. The following questions will help you:

1. Does my vision still feel right?
2. Does it need strengthening?
3. Is it clear enough?
4. Has my experience in the past year said anything to me about what is really important to me?
5. Do I want to revise my vision?

Take your five life dreams (page 44), and ask yourself the same five questions against each dream in turn. Give yourself 10 minutes for the reviewing of each dream — a total of 50 minutes overall. At the end of this time you will have five revised or reaffirmed dreams. It is now time for lunch!

If you are doing this with others, eg with your spouse, or management team you should allow an extra six minutes per dream statement, ie another half hour in total.

In the afternoon the time should be given over to a review of your life areas (see page 53). Allow at least three hours for this, but you may wish to allocate the time preferentially to, for example, 'family' and 'work', at the expense of 'neighbours' and 'social'. Whatever approach you choose, set your time and stick to it.

Use the twelve questions (page 107) to help you through this section and make sure you have a break mid afternoon. I work with many management teams who carry out the above exercise on an annual or more frequent basis. In the book *People and Organisations Interacting* there is a detailed description of a management team which carried out three major reviews in eighteen months using a variation of my approach to review. It worked for them and it could work for you.[23]

Before you complete this round, reach for your diary and book a review day now!

Interval Training Exercise — All Weights
Use the list of questions (page 107) to review your performance against one of your dreams.

Round Nine

Conserving Your Energy

No course on effective living and time management could be complete without a consideration of energy – particularly as we are using the analogy of the boxing ring. The successful fighter knows how to conserve energy.

You will have seen some boxers who bob around the ring, dancing round their opponents, never at rest for the whole of the contest. The great Muhammed Ali was called the Butterfly for this very reason. Other boxers seem almost rooted to the canvas. Most fighters start off with a lot of energy looking for a quick finish but have to slow down in the middle rounds only to burst forth in a fury of activity as the final rounds approach.

What kind of fighter are you? Can you pace yourself or have you only too speeds – full speed and dead stop?

Energy is simply your capacity to do work. If you can work you have energy; if you cannot you haven't! In mechanics there are two kinds of energy – kinetic and potential.

Kinetic energy is the energy you have because of your movement: the faster you move the greater your energy. Potential energy is the energy you possess because of your position. For example, you possess more potential energy at the top of the stairs than you do at the bottom.

Clearly the more energy you have available, the more work you can get through, and the more you can achieve in terms of your targets. So let us consider for a moment the sources of energy available to you and how you might increase your energy reserve. The diagram overleaf shows the major sources of energy available to us.

Sources of Energy

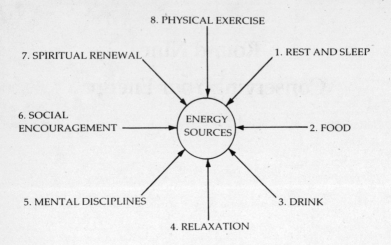

The diagram shows eight sources of energy; there are others. Not everyone will be able to make use of all the sources of energy. For example, if you are disabled then physical exercise may be a very limited source of energy renewal. But let's examine each of the eight before you attempt to assess your current energy sources.

Rest

Rest is your greatest friend when it comes to managing your energy reserves. Many of the world's leaders have punishing daily schedules, from early morning working breakfasts, to late-night dinners and after-dinner speeches. How do they manage it? Many of them rest in the afternoon for 20 to 30 minutes. Each day, fitted around their public appointments, is their private rest time. If seeing the day through is a problem for you then build in a rest period.

In the hotter parts of the world the 'siesta' is a common feature of life.

Those at home are much freer to choose when to have their rest. If that applies to you, take it when you need it and do not feel guilty about putting your feet up; having a rest is a way of improving on the quality and quantity of your activity in the next part of the day.

Sleep

One of my most bizarre counselling sessions took place in the fast lane of a highway in Northern Europe. I was out in the country to give a seminar on the effective use of time and was being driven back to the city by one of the local organisers.

He drove very fast, talked incessantly and seemed to pay very little attention to road signs, road users, mirrors or signals. For the sake of my own stress levels, I asked if he had had many accidents during the bad winters.

He eased his foot off the accelerator as he launched into how busy his life was, and how useful the seminar had been and how much more he would now be able to do. But, he added, he had one problem that I had not touched upon. I hung on, as we swung into the centre lane narrowly missing a timber wagon.

'Sleep,' he continued, 'I have a problem with sleep.'

'Ah!' I replied 'You find it difficult to sleep? Perhaps it is because you are so tensed up when you drive.' He eased back again on the accelerator and said, 'No, No. I sleep too long! I waste time sleeping!'

During the remainder of the journey I explored with him his problem. He was trying to reduce his sleeping time to two hours per night! He had come across some leaders from the Far East on one of his frequent trips abroad and these men and women slept for no more than four hours. My driver was determined to outdo them. I relaxed a bit: at least there was no risk of him falling asleep at the wheel with that kind of target!

It was the idea of regular rest periods which appealed to him as a way of meeting his target. It seems to be working for him – and he hasn't fallen asleep on a highway yet!

Our sleeping patterns are as varied as our faces, but we all need sleep. Sleep is the great restorer of energy. If your energy levels are low then get to bed early. Do not waste time watching TV. Watch the late news if you must, but be in bed by 10.35 – sooner if possible. It seems that the old saying, 'Early to bed, early to rise,' does fit with good time management techniques. You will need on average eight hours sleep per night – more if you regularly feel weary. It's possible to do with much less sleep – for a limited time, but the fact that sleep deprivation is a technique used to break people's physical and mental condition should be sufficient warning to my driver friend and you, that you take a big risk with your health if you cut back on your sleep.

For those who have difficulty sleeping, I will provide some help when I deal with relaxation and mental discipline.

Food

What you eat is the fuel for your body. Quantity is not the most important factor. A heavyweight boxer will eat much more than a lightweight, but both have to go the fifteen rounds. However, eating too much can be a problem. Weightwatching has become international big business. Books and programmes about food and health abound; clearly many of us overeat. What about you? Are you too heavy? There are tables which give you the ideal weight for your height, but a better indicator is how you feel. If you are readily out of breath, easily tired and at the same time heavier than the guidelines then it is likely that you would benefit from losing a few pounds. Your symptoms may be indicators of some other problem, but whether that is so or not, losing a few pounds can only be helpful.

As I said, quantity is not the main factor in terms of energy source, it is the quality that counts. Most developed countries have a diet high in junk food — and our eating habits are deteriorating. If you suffer from low energy then change your diet. Go for:

More
Fresh fruit
Fresh vegetables
Mineral and vegetable
fats
Meat and fish
Soups
Eggs
Wholegrain products

Less
Tinned fruit
Processed vegetables and
meats
Animal fats
Sausages
Sweets
Chips
Pasta

In the book *10 Day Clean-Up Plan*[24], Leslie Kenton has a chapter entitled 'Move toward Energy'. This readable all round approach to restoring your body's balance is well worth perusing.

Drink

We are more than 75% fluid! Despite the impression that we get of being solid 'bone and muscle', we are in fact mostly water! Hence, the importance of what we drink.

Most of us drink too little and what we do drink is often not all that helpful! Swap your coffees and teas for fruit juices; and for every glass of wine or pint of beer, take two glasses of water. Start the day with a cup of hot water with a slice of lemon. Avoid fizzy drinks and fruit drinks with artificial colouring (read the labels). Drink more. A higher intake of fluids will help keep your system 'flushed' clean; a clean system requires less energy to keep functioning than a clogged system — hence there is more energy available for action.

Relaxation

If your energy levels are low then a few moments relaxation will help restore a few of those drained power cells. Relaxation takes many forms. You can relax, for instance, through:

- breathing exercises
- muscle tone exercises
- meditation
- bathing

Clearly it's not always possible for you to strip off and have a hot herbal bath every time you feel your energy low — so you need to develop a method of relaxation which you can use in as many situations as possible. Breathing exercises, muscle tone exercises and meditation fit into this category. The first two are easy to learn; meditation can prove a little harder. Let's start with breathing exercises.

When I ask people what they do to relax, I usually get a list of sports and pastimes! 'Oh, I play golf,' or 'I am a pot holer,' or ' I hang-glide'. These are all very useful but they require quite a lot of equipment and energy. Breathing exercises require very little time and energy and no equipment, and are a good way of recharging your batteries.

How does it work? Breathing supplies oxygen to our bloodstream which in turn feeds the multitudinous cells of the various organs and functioning elements of our body. With insufficient oxygen our efficiency declines, we become weary and our muscles ache. Proper breathing delivers energy-sustaining oxygen and expels the waste — particularly carbon dioxide. Poor breathing causes a high level of noxious substances in our blood stream which in turn further reduces our energy potential.

In Round Four we considered some of the problems of living in a divided world. Many of our breathing problems arise because we see ourselves as divided into parts — head, chest, abdomen, arms, legs etc. We talk about our legs being tired as though they were almost disconnected from the rest of us. And most people think of their lungs as being the part of them that breathes, forgetting that our lungs cannot function properly if our posture is wrong, or if our abdomen cannot respond, or our nasal passages are blocked, or even if our clothing is too tight.

How do you know whether your breathing is correct? Correct breathing involves the whole body, it is called diaphragmatic breathing.

It's not hard to find out whether you are breathing diaphragmatically. To check place your right hand on your chest and note its rise and fall as you breathe. Next you move your hand to your stomach and continue to breathe. If as you breathe in your abdomen contracts as your chest expands, then you aren't breathing correctly.

It doesn't take long to learn how to breathe diaphragmatically. (If you can pronounce it, you can do it!) Correct breathing can be carried out in five steps:

1. Sit or stand up straight, draw your shoulders down and back.
2. Breathe in through your nose letting your abdomen swell as you count slowly to five.
3. Continue inhaling through your nose for a further count of five but this time let your chest expand.
4. Hold your breath for a further count of five.
5. Exhale through your mouth gently while you count to ten.

Repeat this five times, concentrating on your stomach and step 2, since this is the most unfamiliar part of the exercise.

This exercise should be carried out when you rise every morning and at any time in the day when you feel tense or at a low energy level.

There are cassette recordings available which are designed to help you improve your breathing and to help you relax through muscle control.[25]

Mental Discipline
Weariness is often more a psychological symptom than a physical symptom. One source of energy is our mind — it can

provide us with an attitude of enthusiasm and motivation which will carry us through those periods of low energy.

Positive thinking is badly needing to be rediscovered in our society. Most news is bad news, most situations are problem situations, we fear tomorrow rather than hope for it.

When you are tired, think strong! I have had in my office for a number of years a picture of the climber Doug Scott on a vertical ice face on Everest. Whenever I feel that I cannot cope, I look at this picture and tell myself that I have all that it takes. So have you. Remember the Ojibway Indian in Round One. When you are weary lift your voice in an everyday song of thanks for what you have done! (See page 36.)

Take control of your mind! Force it to think on those things which give you energy and inspire you, rather than those things which drain your determination and depress you.

Social Encouragement

There are those people in this world who for some reason or other seem to be followed by gloom and despondency. One of the characters in a book called *So Long and Thanks For All the Fish* is a long distance lorry driver.[26] Everywhere this man goes it rains — you know the kind of person I'm sure — eternal pessimist.

On the other hand there are those who always seem to come up smiling no matter how difficult their situations are. Five minutes with them and you feel the sun has never stopped shining.

Their presence enriches you and encourages you. If you have such friends cherish them. If you haven't, cultivate people like this: They are such powerful sources of energy renewal for others that you cannot miss them.

Spiritual Renewal

In his book *Managing Yourself* Stephen B Douglas begins by stating a number of 'spiritual prerequisites' for personal time management.[27] He shows that guilt is an energy drainer and that a sense of forgiveness is a powerul energy renewer.

Whatever your philosophy or faith, one fact is central: you have a dimension that is not physical. That dimension, if not cared for or recognised, will deprive you of one of the potential sources of energy; and therefore, since you are a total person, your overall effectiveness is diminished.

How can you care for your spiritual dimension and ensure that its potential is available to you? Prayer is the power line at the source of all spiritual energy. The evidence of generation after generation of those who have found this spiritual dimension should not be ignored.

Prayer may be an unfamiliar experience for you, but as with your breathing the more you practice it the easier it becomes. A helpful booklet is 'Meditative Prayer' by Richard Foster.[28] Check back to your life targets (Page 53), do any reflect your spiritual self?

Physical Exercise

If you are fit enough to exercise regularly, then do so: jogging, swimming, tap dancing, aerobics, walking ... Exercise on a daily basis; a weekly visit to the squash courts or the annual golf outing is not enough! Three minutes a day is worth more than three hours every Saturday.

If you feel fatigued, try lying down on the floor and breathing properly for five minutes, or lightly jog on the spot for three. Inactivity is one of the greatest killers of our time; you are never too old to keep fit!

Assessing Your Energy Sources

We have considered eight sources of energy on which you may draw. Do you make the best use of the energy available to you? Here is a table which will help you assess how well you are using your energy potential.

For each of the eight major sources of energy you are asked to rate the amount of consideration you give to it, on a scale of 8 to 1. For example, if you are particular about your diet and try always to eat wholesome, balanced meals, then score yourself 8. But if you think that food is there solely to be enjoyed and do not discriminate in what you eat or the amounts, then score yourself 1.

Do the same for all eight energy sources and enter your total score at the foot of the table.

Rate Yourself On Your Energy Sources

Source of Energy	Amount of Consideration I Give to It		Score
	A lot Insufficient		
1. Rest and Sleep	8 7 6 (5) 4 3 2 1		5
2. Food	8 (7) 6 5 4 3 2 1		7
3. Drink	(8) 7 6 5 4 3 2 1		8
4. Relaxation	8 7 6 5 4 (3) 2 1		3
5. Mental Disciplines	8 7 6 5 (4) 3 2 1		4
6. Social Encouragement	8 7 6 5 (4) 3 2 1		4
7. Spiritual Renewal	8 (7) 6 5 4 3 2 1		7
8. Physical Exercise	8 7 6 5 4 (3) 2 1		3
		Total	

If you scored 50 and over, you are obsessed with your state of health. Relax and live for a change!

If you scored 40 to 49 — well done and keep it up.

If you scored 30 to 39 — more thought is needed in all the areas.

If you scored 20 to 29 — you could be much more effective by developing some energy disciplines.

If you scored 10 to 19 — you run a high risk of burning yourself out. If you scored below 10 — would you like some help to turn over the page?!

Sappers of Energy

We have considered how you might tap your energy sources more effectively. But it will not help us very much if we do not plug our energy drains.

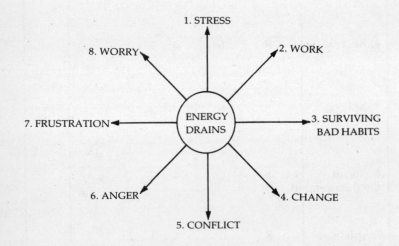

Stress

All change brings with it a degree of stress. 'Good' changes and 'bad' changes bring with them the need for readjustment. Readjustment requires effort and uses energy. Effort and energy involve pressures and forces. Pressures and forces introduce stress.

We hear much about stress and stress-induced illness. A more accurate term would be strain. Our lives could not be lived without pressure — air pressure, blood pressure, brake pad pressure, doorbell pressure. All of these put our physical system under stress. But these types of stress have beneficial consequences: None of us would be without those pressures. However, there are other pressures which produce stress in our lives and which we can well do without.

Excessive demands of work on mind, body and spirit can produce physical, spiritual and mental stress: pressure which hurts; forces which take us beyond our capacity to recover quickly. This can be illustrated graphically, as shown below.

When we are under low pressure, we are relaxed and the motivation to do much is absent, so we are not efficient in terms of work. When the pressure increases motivation increases and efficiency increases also; but when pressure reaches very high levels, our efficiency and effectiveness falls off and we risk burning ourselves out.

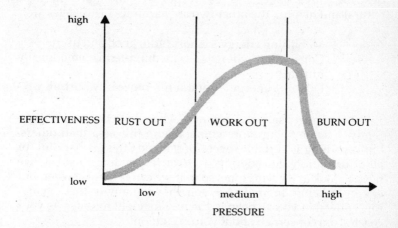

Thus at low levels of pressure our effectiveness is low — ideal for holiday conditions but inappropriate to our normal busy life. We could label this 'rust out.' As the pressure increases, through demands, dead lines or threats, so our responses increase and we become more effective. We can call this 'work out'. But we cannot respond infinitely or indefinitely, there is a point at which our effectiveness begins to decline. This phenomenon has been called 'burn out'. It is particularly prevelant in the helping professions — teaching, counselling, the police, nursing and the church. It seems that a constantly high level of demand is more than the human spirit can stand. If you operate in close proximity to people who place many demands upon you, it is important for you to ensure that you balance these energy drains with appropriate energy sources.

What else can you do when pressure begins to build up? It will help if you understand how you react to pressure. When threatened you react either by fighting back or running away. Those two responses − fight and flight − are the basic defense systems for your body when it is under threat or put under stress. Fight and flight are the primary stress responses; they are natural reactions.

If, however your efforts to fight off the threat are ineffective or you are unable to run away and the threat is maintained, the secondary stress responses of brain and body are triggered off: physical and emotional responses such as a rise in the rate of your heartbeat, changes in your breathing, and feelings of fear, anger, anxiety, distress. These, as we've seen are all energy drainers.

In her book *Stressmanship*, Dr Audrey Livingstone Booth describes three stages of stress response − the first is normal, natural and helpful; the other two are harmful.[29] The stages are:

1. Mobilising energy − short-term, good and useful
2. Consuming energy − medium-term, emotionally hurtful
3. Draining energy − long-term, physically hurtful.

Stress shows itself in different ways and affects people differently − some being more vulnerable in this area than others; but one thing is certain: severe prolonged stress is harmful for all of us. Before considering ways of responding to stress, we need to look at its symptoms so that we can recognise when our energy is being drained. Are you showing any of these symptoms now that you've been in the ring for eight rounds? As your coach, I am concerned about your condition!

Recognising stress

The first step in managing stress is to recognise it. Be aware. Be alert. The following list illustrates some of the features which might indicate that you are suffering from stress. Check yourself as you read the list. Have you:

1. Changed your behaviour patterns by becoming
    - more active?
    - less active?
    - withdrawn?

Yes	No
Yes	No
Yes	No

2. Changed your living pattern in terms of what you
    - eat?
    - drink?
    - how long you sleep?

Yes	No
Yes	No
Yes	No

3. Changed your attitude significantly by becoming
    - more aggressive/passive?
    - unpredictable?
    - less tolerant of uncertainty?

Yes	No
Yes	No
Yes	No

4. Changed your thinking capacity by becoming
    - less able to concentrate?
    - more forgetful?
    - unable to switch off?

Yes	No
Yes	No
Yes	No

5. Noticed more physical problems
    - back problems?
    - headaches?
    - chest pains?
    - digestive problems?

Yes	No
Yes	No
Yes	No
Yes	No

6. Noticed spiritual symptoms (*Church goers only*)
    - loss of spriual 'tone'?
    - loss of spiritual appetite?
    - withdrawal from fellowship?

Yes	No
Yes	No
Yes	No

If you have responded 'yes' 6 or more times, pay particular attention to what I have to say now; if you scored 10 or more yes's then you should go direct to Round Twelve.

Dealing with stress

There are a number of approaches which can be adopted in order to reduce stress, for often we are the major source of our own stress.

Change brings stress, and one way of reducing this is to pace change over a period of time so that too much upheaval doesn't happen all at once. Try to avoid, for example, experiencing all the following changes in a short period of time:

- a new home
- a new location
- a new school
- a new church
- a new job
- new friends
- a new lifestyle
- new eating habits
- new sleeping habits
- new hobbies

As an exercise, list the changes that a retiring couple may experience on moving their home to the coast after 40 years of living in suburbia.

If you cannot phase the rate at which you experience change, a second way of reducing stress is to reduce your response to the demands of change. It is rarely necessary or possible to respond to all the demands placed upon us, yet we often try to do this and then feel guilty about our failure to respond adequately. If you cannot pace the demands on you, then reduce your response to them. For example, a family or an individual under pressure from the demands of creditors, may achieve respite by agreeing to make limited but regular repayments which suit the debtor, thus reducing their response to the demands. I will deal more thoroughly with this way of reducing stress in Round Eleven.

Another technique is to plan your day. Many pressures come from the moment by moment demands of the day. Taking time to plan gives purpose and structure to your time and leads to more effective use of time. By remaining in control you can experience a reduced level of stress and increased level of achievement and satisfaction. So make more use of your daily planning list. (See Round Six).

Settle for improvement

Focusing on success, looking for and building on what works

for you (See Round Eight), can help to offset the distress of failure. Any new venture — whether it's learning to windsurf, or be a mother or father for the first time — offers an opportunity to fail, and may in turn reduce your confidence, willingness to experiment and capacity for learning. Hence, the importance of counterbalancing experiences of failure with a focus on success.

Sometimes the answer is to settle for improvement rather than perfection. This is especially appropriate when you are faced with new situations and unfamiliar tasks. Trying to be a perfectionist in such circumstances usually results in frustration and anger. If you aim instead for an improvement in your performance which is within your present capability, your stress will diminish.

A fifty-two-year-old friend of mine suffered a heart attack and eventually underwent major bypass surgery. There followed a long period of recuperation in which he attempted to push his body further and faster than it could go. His doctor, worried by my friend's exertions gave him a pedometer and instructed him to walk no more than 200 paces each day for the next four weeks.

The invalid was delighted and proceeded to use the pedometer to set new increased targets on a daily basis! After three weeks of increasing his daily walks by 25 steps, he suffered a major setback and was hospitalised for more than two months!

Do not drive yourself beyond your limit! Listen to what your body says to you. Pay attention when it says, 'I'm tired. I've had enough for one day.'

Stress levels will build up throughout the day unless you make periods of quiet and relaxation. These periods should not simply be physical, although physical relaxation will help your total state. The doctor needs a break from the emotional stress of sitting in a chair dealing with patients. The tutor needs to rest his mind after two hours with the post graduate study group. The clergyman needs to be restored after a period of intense counselling. The shop steward needs a break after negotiations. You need a break after each period of effort.

After a period of stress, your body will gradually revert to equilibrium but in your normal day there is often insufficient opportunity to be still; so before your level of stress has fallen to the equilibrium, another stress factor is applied: the alarm shocks us awake; the cat and dog have a fight in the kitchen; the children argue over whose turn it is to have the plastic soldier/car/animal from the breakfast cereal; the milk gets spilt; you cannot find the car keys; there is a flat tyre; a son/daughter has been out in the car and emptied the petrol tank; and that's all before you arrive at work, or start your daily round at home!

128

Let's check you out against the full range of energy drains:

Stress
Work
Surviving bad habits
Change
Conflict
Anger
Frustration and
Worry

Mark each statement in the list below with a tick if it definitely applies to you, 'x' if it definitely does not apply to you, and with a 0 if it applies sometimes.

Where Does Your Energy Go?

1. My work is physically demanding — 0
2. I am somewhat overweight — ✓
3. My life is full of change at the moment — 0
4. I have frequent quarrels at home — X
5. I tend to lose my temper — ✓
6. I find difficulty in completing tasks — ✓
7. I am a worrier — 0
8. I take sedatives — X
9. I have a lot of mental activity in my work — ✓
10. I drink more than four glasses of alcoholic drink in one day — X
11. I am in my forties — X
12. I do a lot of negotiating/selling/persuading — X
13. I am easily angered — 0
14. I am easily discouraged — 0
15. I don't sleep well — 0
16. My life is under pressure — ✓
17. My work is very varied — ✓
18. I have to entertain a lot — 0
19. I travel internationally — X

20. I have trouble with my neighbours

21. I have strong beliefs

22. I know what I want to do but often cannot do it

23. I get uptight and cannot enjoy my food

24. I smoke more than 10 cigarettes/cigars a day

25. My work is quite boring

26. I rarely get more than 6 hours' sleep

27. I am in my twenties or sixties

28. I enjoy a good argument

29. I prefer to confront rather than avoid conflict

30. I often wish I was someone else

31. I often worry about the future

32. My weight varied by more than 14 pounds last year.

Score yourself   3 for every √   *27*
                 1 for every ×   *10*
                 2 for every 0   *26*

(The reason that you score 1 even though it is not you is that you will come across people like that quite regularly — and you will find them a drain on your energies!)

Now transfer your scores on to the following table. This will help you to assess the level and nature of your energy drains. It will also indicate those areas in which you need to take action to stop the outflow of valuable energy.

Energy Drain	Scores from Statements				Totals
Stress Your Score	8	16	24	32	
Work Your Score	1	9	17	25	
Bad Habits Your Score	2	10	18	26	
Change Your Score	3	11	19	27	
Conflict Your Score	4	12	20	28	
Anger Your Score	5	13	21	29	
Frustration Your Score	6	14	22	30	
Worry Your Score	7	15	23	31	

So now you have some idea of your energy inputs and outputs as represented by your scores on the energy sources table, (page 121), and the energy drain questionnaire results, (page 128). But how do they balance out? Transfer your results to the graph overleaf. To do this mark your energy sources score on the vertical column at the left hand side of the graph and mark your energy drain score on the base line. Then draw a horizontal line from your source score to meet a vertical line from your drain score. Where do they meet?

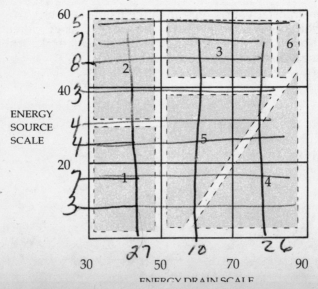

ENERGY SOURCE SCALE

ENERGY DRAIN SCALE

There are six main areas on the graph:

Area 1: The wake up zone
Area 2: The under utilised zone
Area 3: The effective living zone
Area 4: The disatisfied zone
Area 5: The transition zone
Area 6: The super-risk zone

If you are in the wake up zone then I presume someone is reading this book to you or you have so much time on your hands that you have nothing else to do. Start living before you fossilize!

If you are in the under-utilised zone you have a lot more energy than you need — try spreading some around; the world needs your energy!

The effective living zone is where we all want to be — keep a place for us, if you're there!

Area 4 residents should beware. You are in danger of depleting your energy resources in a serious manner. You are living too fast and not paying enough attention to your own needs. Slow down.

Area 5 people are often in transition — neither one thing nor another. Commit yourself to an energy generation programme.

Area 6 people are probably reading this because, on flicking through the pages their eyes were caught by the graph. Why don't you buy the book and go through it? The experience will probably add a few years to your lifespan.

Interval Training Exercise
After a round like this who has got energy for exercises? Sit back and practice your breathing for three minutes!

Round Ten
Involving Your Team

Let me give a special word of encouragement to you if you have come straight from the Pre-fight Check List having scored over 200 points. You join with those who have already gone nine rounds but your strength is in your willingness to follow helpful suggestions, such as starting to read a book two thirds of the way through! Well done! Welcome also to readers who haven't enough time to complete Round Four at this moment.

Time management is a team game. You cannot significantly improve your use of time unless you involve others. It is very true that we are not islands; we do not live in isolation. Many of the demands which we find so burdensome come, strangely enough from our family our friends and our neighbours. It is not that we don't value them but they seem to ask so much at times.

Now is the time for you to ask something in return.

People Need People
People need people but asking for help does not come easy. We find it hard to ask for help for various reasons. We have been taught that seeking for help is something that we shouldn't do; that it's a weak thing to do — and we mustn't be weak or be seen to be weak, that we should be self-sufficient and independent; that because it's more blessed to give than to receive, it's wrong to do *any* receiving! Also, we don't believe that others would understand our needs or — even if they did — be able or willing to help us.

I once heard an African leader appealing to the rich nations to help the poorer ones to grow to maturity. He spoke of the way missionaries had come to his country to preach about the Christian God: a God who is a giver and who wants his children to be givers too. But, he said, Africa is not able to give because the West will not receive. He went on to say that although Africa depends on the wealthier nations for a certain amount of material aid, she and other third world countries have much to teach the so-called developed nations — about such matters, for instance, as family life, old age, the community, youth; but we won't receive what they have to offer, to the detriment of our society with its breakdown in family and community life, its frustrated youth and so on.

People can help one another in all sorts of ways. In terms of time management, people could help you to create your own space and to achieve your dreams and targets.

Groups

We group people as family, friends, bosses, peers, subordinates, colleagues, fellow committee members, and so on. I would like you to list, in column one of the chart opposite, all the groups to which you belong. In a survey I conducted in Liverpool, I found that, on average, people see themselves as belonging to five groups. As an extreme exception, one minister listed membership of 38 groups!

Now in column two, write the number of hours per week that you spend with each group. If you have put down 'family' as a group, you may find it easier to break this down into subgroups, eg spouse and children and parents.

Now in the third column and fourth column I would like you to rate as high, medium or low the value first to yourself (column three) and then to the others (column four) of the time you spend with each group. For example, if you spend three hours a week with the Women's Institute or the bridge team you may rate this time as of low value to you, but of high value to others, because you're good on the committee, a good bridge player, or whatever. Or it may be that you enjoy bridge but are not a good player and go only to make up the foursome. In that case, the value of that time to you may be medium and the value of your time to them may be low.

If you have difficulty in assessing the value to yourself of any group, you might find it helpful to ask yourself if the time with the group contributes to any of your priorities. (See page 65.)

Sorting out Priorities

Now that you have filled in the chart, what are you to make of what you have written and how should you respond?

Column One	Column Two	Column Three	Column Four
Groups to Which I Belong	Time/Week	Value to Me	Value to Them
1.			
2.			
3.			
4.			
5.			
6.			
7.			

The groups against which you have written 'high' in columns three and four will obviously be good groups for you to continue to be involved with. Probably this won't apply to more than two or three groups.

You should seriously consider withdrawing from those groups against which you've written 'low' in both the third and fourth column. Perhaps next time you meet these groups, you could explain that you are working on a programme to improve your use of time and ask them to bear with you while you withdraw for a while to organise your priorities. If your low/low assessment is correct, you will receive a positive response.

What about groups against which you wrote 'low' in column three and 'medium' in column four? See whether you can halve the time you spend with these groups. If this isn't possible, you should probably withdraw from them altogether. You have only one life and you want to live it to the full!

Against one or two groups you might have written 'low' in column three and 'high' in column four. You should probably stay with these groups, but work on trying to improve their value to you, by — for example — changing the time, frequency or content of the group activities to better suit your needs and priorities. If the group won't change, then it is likely that you have over-estimated your value to it! So withdraw or reduce your commitment — and see what happens.

Interdependence

Interdependence in relationships is the ideal mix between independence and dependence.

It involves, for one thing, sharing and being open to advice and comment. I suggest that next time you meet with your 'high-high' group, you explain to the members that you are developing your time management skills and that you need their help. Those who have come straight from the Pre-fight Check List, because they scored 200 plus points, should share their results with their high-high group.

Specifically, you could ask the other members of the group to review your progress with you regularly — at least once a month for the next six months. Ask them for observations on how you spend your time and on how you might reduce the amount of time you spend on less profitable activities.

The following list of questions might help others to help you:

1. What do I do that seems to you to be inefficient?
2. In what ways do I waste your time?

3. Can you suggest ways in which I could organise myself better?
4. How could we work together more effectively?
5. Do I get in the way or get involved when I shouldn't?

You will find that members of groups which value your contribution will be only too willing to share their ideas with you. And they may want to borrow this book when you have finished with it!

If it's clear from the way you filled in the chart (page 135) that you are not a member of the high-high group that could help you with your time management problems — take heart: you are not alone. My own research suggest that 95 per cent of people experience time pressures and more than half of these experience time related stress — that is, so much pressure that it hurts! So what can you do? If you are not a member of a 'high-high' group, then create one. Find yourself two people who are also experiencing 'time squeeze', and suggest that you work on the problem together. Introduce them to this book and meet for an hour once a fortnight to discuss progress. The power of the small group to support its members is well known and is widely used in counselling. The fastest growing movement in Europe is the House Church Movement, characterised by small dedicated groups linked by a common purpose and ready to support each other.

Relating to others on the basis of interdependence and mutuality also involves a willingness to encourage others to take responsibility when this is appropriate and to discourage the wrong sort of dependency. I was once dining with the managing director of a very successful international business. We were eating in a private dining room, overlooking a private lake dotted with (no doubt private) ducks! My companion, who had been managing director for 25 years, was within three years of retirement and had no successor in sight. For a quarter of a century he had led the organisation and made all the major decisions — creating not only the dependent ducks outside but also the dependent team inside. What should he do? My response was direct 'Begin now to reduce dependency on you. Give your management team the responsibility and authority to run their own departments.'

On another occasion, I was having a meal on a different table, with a different client but the same problem. This time my client was a worn-out widow who was struggling hard to keep a home together for her three boys. She felt she couldn't go on. She told me: 'I've struggled to keep the family together for 12 years, ever since Jack died, but it's too much now — what with the work and the shopping and the housework and the cooking. The boys eat such a lot. But then they do at that age don't they?'

'What age?' I prompted. 'Well young Jack will be 26 next birthday and Tommy is 24 and Simon's 19'!! Perhaps you can imagine what I said! At their age, the boys ought to have stopped leaning on Mum!

Now what about you? What are you doing for others that they could do for themselves or could do without?

Is there anything the children can do at home? Then organise them to do it! They are not too young to learn the value of time, not least the value of your time. Is there anything your ageing mother or father can do? If so, let them do it! It will give them a sense of value and purpose which, all too often, is missing for the elderly.

In the club, church, society or institute, what are you doing that a younger person could do? Give them the job if you have the authority to do so; otherwise suggest it to those who do have the authority.

In the work place, delegation is the word. It's essential for encouraging, developing, rewarding and testing others, and for ensuring that the manager has time to do those things which only he can and should do. Check again your score in the questionnaire about the barriers to delegation (page 96).

There is one great incentive that you can use to help yourself in your fight for a more effective use of time. It is the incentive which comes from making a commitment to others. Tell them what your time management targets are: that you hope to finish this book in a week or a month, or whatever; and that you would like to share with them the things you have learned and applied. Why not phone someone and arrange to meet for coffee or lunch for that very purpose today?

Some readers will now be out of sequence having come here direct from the Pre-fight Check List. A word to them, as they return to Round One (page 33). You will find that those around you will be ready, willing and able to help you to become more organised. I suggest that you write down the names of the first two people whom you will approach for help with the management of your time and life. Remember that time management is a team game.

Interval Training Exercise for All Weights

Make the following commitment, by filling in the names.

I feel the following two people should be able to help me form my 'high-high' time management team.

Name 1 _____

Name 2 _____

I will contact them and share with them the five questions on page 136. I will also seek their help to review my progress once a month for the next six months.

PS I will also ensure that one of them is a source of social encouragement – as described on page 119.

Round Eleven

On The Ropes

Old Time, in whose bank we deposit our notes,
Is a miser who always wants guineas for groats.
He helps all his customers still in arrears
By lending them minutes and charging them years.[30]

Despite all that you are learning and despite all the successes you now have under your belt, there will be times when the pressure on your time builds up to unmanageable levels. There will be too much to do and not enough time to do it. You will be on the ropes, and the opposition will not back off. What should you do? The answer is simply 'Do what you can do and don't worry about what you can't do.' You may retort, 'Easier said than done!' Well that is true − initially, but once you have learned the technique of Time Budgeting you may find it easier done than said!

Time Budgeting
We are all aware of what financial budgeting is all about. As Mr Micawber said: 'Annual income one pound, annual expenditure nineteen shillings and sixpence − the result happiness. Annual income one pound, annual expenditure one pound and six pence − result misery.'[31]

As far as time budgeting is concerned, happiness would be to manage everything and have time left. But how many of us budget our time?

We prepare holiday budgets, pocket money budgets, budgets for presents, cars and new household appliances. Before buying anything, we open our wallet or purse and decide whether or not we can afford it. If we can − fine! If we can't we must go for something which costs less or wait until we have more money. Similarly, when we are short of time, we can leave the task until we have more time, or cut back our aspirations and give the task less time than we would ideally have liked to give it.

Why is it that people feel good about cutting back on expenditure — it's good stewardship, responsible living, etc — but feel guilty about cutting back on time?

For many people it is a matter of pride. They want the best; they want to do their best; only the best is good enough! Yet in the area of finance they are prepared to save, to wait or to accept that the best for them is not the best available. We all have our dream holidays, dream houses, dream cars ... but these dreams don't (or shouldn't) stop us being very pleased with this year's actual holiday, car and house. We are satisfied because they are probably the best we are able or willing to afford at this time. This very practical approach to finance unfortunately is not often extended to the realm of time. When we don't have time for the best, we get worked up, and feel angry, frustrated, disappointed or guilty. Why? Because we are not prepared to settle for second best, even although second best is quite good enough for the situation. The best has become the enemy of the good.

A group of deacon's met once a month, in different church members' homes. Proceedings were usually fairly long and drawn out — except at Mrs Levin's! There things were very different. The meetings were business like, well ordered, to the point and over in little more than half the usual time. Why? Because Mrs Levin's pastries were second to none in quality or quantity! The deacons' delight at the result of her preparations never failed to be reflected in the face of Mrs Levin. Her tired eyes would glow with pleasure at the praises. She would brush aside a strand of greying hair, saying, 'Its the least I can do.'

But it wasn't. It was the most she could do and far more than she should have done. Other duties were neglected, other responsibilities were pushed aside as her turn to host the meeting came around. Without freezer or microwave, preparation was a hassle which affected her family for a week prior to the visit. She wanted to produce the best — not merely the best possible given her other commitments — but the very best. And so she robbed time from her husband, her children, her friends and even herself.

The situation came to light during a pastoral visit. Mrs Levin was found to be suffering from her nerves. The pastor assessed what was happening and issued the following request to all hostesses: 'In order to increase time for prayer during the deacons' meetings the deacons would appreciate it if the hostesses would provide only cups of tea and plain digestive biscuits.' After this, the meetings improved greatly and so did Mrs Levin's health. Often you are on the ropes because that is where you have put yourself.

Your Time Budgeting

In Round Four you identified targets in each of the main areas of your life — family, marriage, work, church, leisure, neighbours, self. But you did not attempt to budget your time against them. Now you need to do that. You are under pressure, with your back to the ropes, unable to do all you want to do or to reach the standards you want to reach. You therefore have a choice. Will you leave some items undone or reduce the quality and quantity of what you do?

Fill in columns two and three on the weekly personal time budget table below. Under 'present allocation' (column two), write the time you actually spend on your life's priorities. If you find this hard, refer to your time-use table in Round One (page 34). Under 'desired allocation' (column three), write the time you would like to spend on your life's priorities. We will deal with how to move from column three to column four shortly.

Area of Life	Present Allocation hours/week	Desired Allocation hours/week	Example hours/week
1 Time with Family			10
2 Time with Partner			16
3 Time to Work			60
4 Time for Church/ Devotions			12
5 Time for Relaxation			2
6 Time for Neighbours			2
7 Time for Community			2
8 Time for Self			2
9 Time for Sleep			56
10 Time for ... eg (House Maintenance)			6
TOTAL	168	168	168

Personal Time Budget Table

Budgeting under Pressure —

When you are under pressure — in the office with a plane to catch and several letters to write, or at home with a meal to prepare and the children to collect you can relieve the situation by:

Asking the Right Questions

List what has to be done. (Yes, actually take time to write it down!) Then check each item against the following questions:

1. Must it be done?
2. Must it be done by me?
3. Must it be done now?
4. How much time do I have?

For all the items to which you have answered, 'Yes', 'Yes' and 'Yes', budget some time bearing in mind your answer to the fourth question. Then do the job, sticking to your budget.

This may mean that instead of a three page letter you write three paragraphs, three lines, or even three words (Will write soon!). It may mean that you stop off at the Chinese take-away or that you use a ready made meal rather than preparing that crown of lamb with apricot soufflé.

It will mean that you will not have time to do all that you would like to have done, and that what you do won't be up to the standard that you are capable of. But you can still call this your best if you do the best you can in the time available.

Being Determined

When you have your back to the ropes, you especially need the first of the four ingredients of a fuller life: determination (See page 27). Deal firmly with the two opponents who have put you in the difficult position — you and others.

Leaving Tasks Undone

Here are some guidelines for your thought and action. They should help you to see what tasks should be left undone or done differently or postponed or delegated.

1. If, when you ask about a proposed task, 'What will happen if I don't do it?' the answer is, 'Nothing,' then leave that task undone and don't worry about it!

2. If not doing the task will mean more work for you another time, then try to reschedule it to a time when, as far as you can gauge, you will not be under pressure.

3. If not doing the task will affect another person, then see whether someone else can do it or, if not, whether the task could be reduced or postponed. (Could someone else make the cake? Would a bought cake do instead? Could the deadline for the report be changed or would a summary do instead?)

4. If someone will be disappointed if you don't do something (eg take the family to the cinema or for a meal out), try to arrange to do the same thing (or perhaps something even better) at a different, less pressurised date.

5. Take to heart the advice of a chaplain I heard, who told a group of people working on time management that one of the most powerful strategies for dealing with time pressures is prayer. He said, 'Do what you can, and what you cannot do, commit to God.'

Do not try to work out 'why' you have your back to the ropes; concentrate on what has to be done. There will be plenty of time later to see why things built up as they did.

Not Being Afraid to Say 'No!'

Some people are afraid to say, 'No' to others. Are you like that? If so, find out from the list below why you find it hard to say, 'No.'

I do not like to say 'No' because:

1. People may be offended.
2. They may not ask me again.
3. I like people to think that I can cope.
4. I would rather say 'Yes'.
5. I like to appear helpful.
6. I feel guilty.
7. People need me.
8. People may be disappointed.
9. I may be the only one who can help.
10. It is my job to say, 'Yes'.

The higher your score, the more you will find yourself overloaded with that rope pressing very hard from behind!

Different ways of saying, 'No'

There are many ways of refusing to do something or turning someone down. Here are some of them:

1. If only you had asked me sooner, I'd have been delighted but ...
2. I am fully committed at the moment but will you remember me next time round?'
3. I am in such demand at the moment that I could not really do justice to what you need, but my planning gets easier next week/month/year. Is that any use to you?'
4. I'd love to do that for you. Could I ask you to pick up the children/visit mother in the hospital/cut my grass for me, otherwise I'll have no free time at all this week?
5. Thank you for asking. I am otherwise engaged then, but have you thought of asking Mrs ...
6. I always feel bad about saying, 'No'. It makes me feel guilty. Please forgive me, but I just have no time for additional commitments that week.'
7. I'm very poor at that; you need someone who could do it better.'
8. I'm working on a project at the moment. Please ask me another time.
9. Yes, I'll be delighted to help but the only time I can do that would be ...
10. No I couldn't do all that, but if I did this bit then you could do the rest couldn't you?

If you can't think of a gracious response, say a simple, 'No – sorry', rather than taking on a job that you have no time to do, that does not fit in with your priorities and won't be done to your usual standards.

Interval Training Exercise for Those on the Ropes

Heavyweights
Write your resignations from half your committees or withdraw from activities which take up at least three hours per week.

Middleweights
Make a list of all those duties and responsibilities that you would really rather not do. Share the list with your 'high-high' group (see Round Ten) and take their advice.

Lightweights
Ask your high-high group to suggest where you could say, 'No,' more often.

Round Twelve

Healing Your Hurts

Paul phoned just after lunch on Monday. I was surprised: he should have been half way across Africa on a business trip.

'I've been fired, Dave,' he said. There was a long pause.

My friend had become another statistic. Among the country's top 10% of earners, a member of social class B, a father of a large family — five children rather than the average 1.8 — he had now joined the ranks of another elite — the 4,000,000 unemployed of Great Britain in the 1980's.

One of the biggest problems facing many people today is not that there is too much to do and not enough time to do it in, but that there's not enough to do and too much time to do it in! Those affected are the young in inner cities and rural communities, the housewife in anonymous suburbia or high-rise blocks, the retired and elderly in the declining resorts around our coasts, and all those deprived of employment for whatever reason.

This round is for all those who have been hurt either by too much or too little to do. I have met with them in Los Angeles, Nairobi, London and Pitlochry. All over the world, time sick people struggle for survival. Hurt and wounded — some deeply — they need help to restore their lives.

What form does this hurt take? How do you know when you are hurt? What can be done to reduce the damage? These are some of the issues that we will tackle now. It may be that in your own fight for effective living you have come off lightly. In that case this round will help you help others less fortunate.

The table below shows the areas of our personality and being which may be affected by extremes of activity — too much or too little to do. Check for the symptoms of hurt in your life. This table is not comprehensive so add your own symptoms in '6'.

Areas of Life affected	Examples of the hurts of —	
	1. Too much to do	2. Not enough to do
1. Self confidence	Sense of failure and loss of faith	Sense of worthlessness and rejection
2. Motivation	Disillusionment	Boredom
3. Relationships	Breakdown due to neglect	Breakdown due to guilt and lethargy
4. Sense of purpose	Confusion of priorities	Absence of priorities
5. Resilience	Stress build up reduces capacity to handle crises	Absence of energy reduces capacity to respond
6. Other (please complete for yourself)		

Symptoms of Hurt

Designed for Success

When I was a young child my father taught me the power of a positive attitude to living through the example of the railway engine on the gradient. Engines in those days were steam powered and would labour up the hills. The engine driver, track engineers and engine designers were all no doubt certain that the gradient could be climbed. To my father and me, standing on the bridge, engulfed in the noise and smoke of the toiling engine, the outcome seemed very much in doubt. Would it make the top we would always wonder? It always did, and we would cheer and walk on to talk about how relieved the engine would feel as it gathered speed down the decline on the other side of the hill. For me not yet six, the determination of the engine to make the top despite the hindering wagons was a powerful image which has stayed with me throughout my life. 'You can if you think you can,' may not always be true, but 'You cannot if you think you cannot, seems to me to be very true.

My childhood fantasies about struggling engines have been replaced by a belief that we have been designed to be successful − not to be failures. Just as the 0-6-0 had been designed and planned for that journey on the outskirts of Glasgow, so men and women have been designed and equipped for success on the journey through life. This is not vague sentimentalism; it's a scientific and spiritual fact, I believe. Darwin's thoughts on the evolutionary process have been widely accepted and developed by the scientific community, despite the many acts of faith that are required to accept the theory. Darwin said, in effect, that the flora and fauna of this world and the human race were equipped for survival, or we might say − for success.[32] From a scientific point of view we are built for success and are the product of successful evolution.

Christians believe that human beings are made in the image of the successful God of creation. So whether you believe in evolution or not, you are designed for success.

Neither of these views suggests that we will always be winners in every situation but they are perhaps sources of encouragement.

Determination is a quality which is very valuable in helping people to succeed. In the opening pages of *Seconds Away!* I reminded you that only four qualities are needed for success: determination, skill, effort and the right environment. We have spent a lot of time on developing your skill, but determination and effort are yours to give or withhold. In his inspiring book *Jonathan Livingston Seagull*, Richard Bach pictures for us the power of determination as the bird pushes out the boundaries of flying in a never-ending search.[33]

Symptoms of Hurt

We may be designed for success, but many people are not succeeding. They are too badly hurt. What are the symptoms of hurt? One is loss of confidence.

Lost Confidence

I sat on the bed in a small study bedroom in one of England's top public schools. Opposite me, with work books and exam papers between us, sat the son of one of my colleagues. A very clever boy, he had lost his confidence. From exceptional performance in his O levels he now viewed his chances of successful A level performance as very low indeed. He had lost faith in himself, as had his tutors.

Together we talked of success and failure. We looked at what he was doing well and were both encouraged. We looked at what was going badly — time management in the preliminary exams, inability to communicate what was in his head, a growing gap between himself and his tutors and teachers. Then we began to laugh — to laugh at the mistakes, to see the humour in the failure. Slowly he regained perspective and was prepared to recognise his strengths and weaknesses, to bring them out into the open and face them as aspects of himself which could be changed — strengths to be built upon, weaknesses to be overcome.

I left the study room having worked out with him a plan for his target, two A's and a B, and a book to help him study and structure his answers.[34]

We met two months later to check progress. He was a different young man. At that second meeting we detailed a daily plan for the month of May and June, working out what he would do each day: what he would study; how he would relax; even down to what he would eat and drink!

The results? Having almost withdrawn from the course he gained two A's and a B in the summer.

With too much to do you need some help from someone you can talk and laugh with. Finish this Round and go back to Round Ten, and redo the exercise on page 139.

Disillusionment

Another symptom of hurt is a feeling of disillusion. When we have too much to do, because people expect too much from us or we expect too much from ourselves, we are in danger of locking ourselves into a spiral of disillusionment.

This is what happens when we begin with high motivation,

high enthusiasm and high energy, but without having truly counted the cost and worked things out.

First our energy goes. We have taken on more than our resources will stand. Then our enthusiasm goes because progress is too slow and there is so much to be done. Finally our motivation goes and we slip further down a spiral of despair. When our motivation goes and our commitment dies, we look for an escape.

But we have locked ourselves in no one will help us out. No one will share with us. We become blocked and frustrated, unable to perform, unable to escape. In this condition we become apathetic and disillusioned, and if the pressure is maintained we slip further into despair.

Where are you? What can you do?

Round Four in which you dealt with the setting of priorities will be helpful to those of you who need help. Round Ten is also important, but first go to Round Nine, for you will need to find the energy to break out of your despair. Study that round as far as the sources of energy table (page 121). Then move to Round Ten, and from there on you will find hope.

Relationship Breakdown

Poor or fractured relationships are a sign of hurt and can result from poor time management. Working 80-100 hours per week may be the sign of a dedicated employee or member of society but it is frequently a recipe for family turmoil. Such an imbalance of priorities causes resentment and pain.

Complete the time budgeting table from Round Eleven (page 143). Share this with those whose relationship you value but have put at risk by your dedication to one or two areas of your life. Ask for their help to reorientate your priorities, in particular your figures in the 'desired allocation' column.

Confusion of Priorities

When work piles up you are at risk of losing sight of your priorities — tasks which are really important to you and the targets you really wish to achieve. The opening rounds of this book deal with the whole topic of priorities, but for those whose lives are in confusion here is a question. If I could only do one thing today, what would it be?

If now is a suitable time to do that thing — go and do it. When you have done it ask yourself the same question again. If now is not a suitable time for doing the thing — ask yourself this question: 'What is the best use of my time right now?'

Go and do whatever your answer suggested. If the answer to either of these questions was 'Read *Seconds Away!*' then I will be happy to share time with you. But first go and do what you must do, being guided by these two questions. *Au Revoir.* You will be back!

Stress and Crisis

You are not alone if you are stressed. That may not be much comfort for you. However, knowing that most people find ways of effectively dealing with their stress should encourage you. In Round Nine you will find a section on stress control. Read pages 122 to 126 then follow on with the earlier part of that round. But remember that if you are actually in a crisis now, you probably should delay finishing this book. There are more important demands on your time!

We now come to the flipside of the work trap: too much time and not enough to do. What hurts does this situation lead to?

Sense of Worthlessness

With increasing unemployment today, more and more people are experiencing:

- loss of independence
- loss of status
- loss of self-respect
- loss of self-esteem
- loss of normal structures and reference points
- stress
- apathy
- despair

All this can add up to a feeling of worthlessess which colours everything and is very disabling. Work ought not to be equated with worth but unfortunately it often is.

The person who is unemployed for whatever reason – no job available, sickness, disability – needs new structures and reference points. In the early rounds of *Fighting for Time* you will find some help in rediscovering a vision of your life and a sense of your inestimable worth.

Purposelessness

A feeling of purposelessness can result from many causes, including unemployment, and its effects can be as devastating

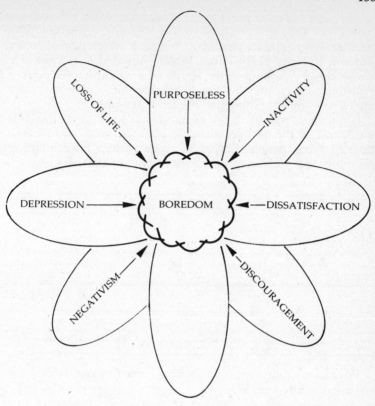

as a feeling of worthlessness. Everything seems pointless, so why bother? The days drag by and the future holds no hope.

The absence of purpose tends to devalue whatever we do. We may enjoy what we are doing, but if it has no purpose other than self-gratification we will soon tire of it. If it has no purpose other than tradition, we may soon tire of it. If Sunday is pointless – we find it boring – and if Monday to Friday are similarly without purpose with long days and restless nights, then Saturday – our one highlight – is come and gone too soon. Like most hurt, if it is not attended to, the sickness of boredom will soon infect other parts of the body. The bored housewife turns to bingo or drink; the bored husband looks around for excitement; the bored teenager experiments with drugs or violence.

One helpful approach to counteract the self-destructive is to engage in some new activity. I often come across parents with bored teenage children; the problem seems to be particularly prevalent among children whose parents' careers take up too much time. I recall one time when a new activity helped. The father complained that his son just lay around all day. The boy would not play golf with his father or bridge with his older brother. I suggested a new sport — one in which neither father nor son had any skill but one which appealed to the son. He chose dinghy sailing! After a year the whole family took a cruising holiday, and the family relationships and enthusiasm are now beyond anything that the father dreamed of.

If you are bored, try experimenting with something new. This week and for the next six weeks, experiment with food, sports, books, places, people. Engage in a new activity now by listing six things that you have never done but might like to try.

1._____

2._____

3._____

4._____

5._____

6._____

Put a date alongside each and bring some fresh air, some fresh experience, into your life.

Guilt

Perhaps the most destructive of the hurts that come from misuse of time is guilt. You feel guilty because you cannot cope or because you can cope but no one will let you — no one will give you a job. You feel that each day is wasted. Multiply the 'golden hours' to the weeks, months and years of the long term unemployed and the sense of loss can be overwhelming.

Horace Mann's beautiful poem captures this regret at the waste of time.

> Lost, yesterday, somewhere between sunrise and
>   sunset,
> Two golden hours
> Each set with sixty diamond minutes
> No reward is offered for they are gone forever.[35]

In the eyes of your friends and neighbours you see accusation or compassion or contempt.

The temptation, when we feel guilty, is to lose ourselves in 'busyness' as an anxiety-avoidance strategy. By filling our hours with activity — any activity — we feel better or we blame others for our problems. These are shallow and short-lived self-deceptions.

It is time to accept the responsibility for living your life well and to the full. Find yourself a new dream — one worthy of your potential and your uniqueness. Round Two is where to start.

No Energy

Lack of energy can be a sign of inner hurt. Round Nine may help you with your energy problem, but energy needs purpose. Better to be without both than to have one without the other! Lots of energy without purpose makes you like a misguided missile — throwing yourself wholeheartedly into profitless activities, while purpose and no energy leads you quickly to frustration. Round Nine will help with the problem.

Healed

A word in closing for those who came to this round with hurts. Only people make you cry was a line from one of the songs in the great musical movie *Paint Your Wagon* . There is much truth in that. Round One of your fight for your life began by identifying the two opponents in your life — yourself and other people. Those two opponents are your only sources of true hurt. To be healed of your wounds takes more than a chapter in a book — it takes people, you and others, but mostly you. Your success in the final rounds of this contest, or in the earlier ones if that is where you are bound, will depend on the action you take.

Act now to begin your own healing processes; take up the portions of this book which are recommended for your particular need.

There are no exercises for this round.

Round Thirteen
Consolidating Your Position

Three more rounds to go! By now you should be able to sense victory. You have had twelve rounds of hard battling but at the end of each, the points have been in your favour. Already you should be feeling stronger. You are not getting in your own way nearly as much, and your team in the corner has begun to get its act together in support of you.

Each round has taught you some new skill and given you some new insight into your own abilities and shortcomings. Round by round, skill by skill, insight by insight, you have grown more able to manage your life and your time with greater effectiveness. You have been developing new life skills: skills which can be applied not only year by year but moment by moment; not only to your life generally, but to particular tasks and challenges in life; skills which are vital in dealing effectively with those major issues of living, those daunting tasks which seem so overwhelming that you are reluctant to start – even if you know where to do so.

Now in terms of consolidating your position – I want to bring many of the skills and lessons together and show how you can apply them to those difficult tasks, and for my illustration I am going to refer to the biggest task ever undertaken, for clearly if these time management principles worked on that job, the skills that you have can be applied to any job.

What was the biggest task ever undertaken? – Creation! The old story from Genesis Chapter 1, the biblical account of the origins of this world of ours. If it is some time since you read that passage take time out to read it again now if you have a Bible to hand. I'm sure you can remember it anyway.

God works for six days and rests on the seventh, and in that time not only is the task completed, but the principles of task management are described: principles, which although you have not been aware of it, you have been learning and practising for the last few days or weeks as you have progressed from round to round through *Fighting for Time*.

Now let's begin on the business of strengthening your position by focusing on the ten basic principles which will help you to succeed, however huge the task.

1. Time management is a daily discipline.
2. Set yourself clear targets.
3. Do only what you alone can or should do.
4. Focus on success.
5. Review regularly.
6. Move forward one step at a time.
7. Share the work.
8. Give space to others.
9. Stop when you have finished.
10. Follow up.

Recognise them? Of course you do! You are beginning to do them all regularly. Let us now see how the principles work out in practice.

Time Management Is a Daily Discipline

If you are really serious about improving your use of time, you must begin today to apply all the concepts and skills that you have developed. This first principle encourages you to do that.

Don't wait until you have a new diary, secretary, office, telephone system or more time. Each day is an opportunity to begin anew. You must commit yourself, daily and wholeheartedly, to the task of effective time management. The point of learning to sing the everyday song in Round One (page 36), was to help you to focus on your daily use of time.

Set Yourself Clear Targets

Nothing causes more task and time difficulties than the absence of clear targets. Without them you cannot establish priorities or plan; you cannot evaluate progress or set boundaries to your activities. So the essential step now is to state clearly what this task is. Write it down. In the opening words of Genesis the task is clearly stated — God sets out to make 'the heavens and the earth.' Five words to describe it. I have worked with people whose great task was described in even fewer words — 'Rebuild our marriage' and in one case one word, 'Gold' — the task of a teenager seeking to win the highest award in the Duke of Edinburgh's Award Scheme.

These targets had to be developed as I have described in Round Three, but what led to success in each of these cases was a clear understanding of what had to be done. Write down your biggest challenge in terms of a target. My biggest challenge is to:

_____

Not only do you need clear targets for your work, but you need clear targets for your activities associated with improved time management. Vital questions in this connection are:

> What is the challenge?
> What do you hope to achieve?
> How long will you take to achieve it?
> How will you know you are making progress?

Without clear answers to these questions, your targets are vague, undefined and of little value; like moving targets, they will elude and frustrate you. In Rounds Three, Four and Five you learned the power of targets, priorities and plans. Now apply this learning to all areas of your life.

Set yourself another target. This time to do with your own effective use of time. What are you aiming for? My target in relation to how I use my time is to:

_____

What You Alone Can or Should Do

There will be certain things that only you can and should do. Focus on these and delegate as many of the other tasks as possible. Your challenge in time management is to create more space in your life for doing those tasks which are real priorities. People press in, via the door, the telephone, or the post, trying to invade your space. We saw in Rounds Nine and Ten how to deal with this invasion.

Keep practising the relevant skills, otherwise you will find yourself caught up in other people's agenda, and the day will end with no space having been found for your priorities: yourself, your family, or your God . . .

Keep remembering to concentrate on those tasks which only you can do. Eighty per cent of our effectiveness lies in 20 per cent of your tasks. Identify that 20 per cent of your tasks which really make the difference, concentrate on them and try to eliminate or delegate the rest.

In Round One you carried out an analysis of how you spend

your time. A typical breakdown might include:

- preparing for work
- handling mail
- telephone calls
- visitors
- travel
- meetings
- planning
- time with family

or for someone working at home:

- organising the family
- cooking
- cleaning
- planning
- shopping
- meetings
- travel
- time with family

Within the spectrum of your activities, there will be some which you classed as important and urgent. They are the priorities: those activities which really made a contribution to the achievement of your targets for the day. And then there were those activities which were classed as low value activities: not urgent and not important. Let us represent the spectrum thus:

LOW VALUE
(not urgent and not
important)

HIGH VALUE
(urgent and important)

Your own analysis is likely to have only about 20 per cent high value activities, as in the diagram below.

0   LOW   40   MEDIUM   80   HIGH   100
     VALUE   VALUE   VALUE

Breakdown of Activity Value Spectrum

It is possible to class the skills required for the range of activities as low, medium or high. High skill tasks involve judgement, experience, influence, etc, whereas low skill tasks might require basic communication or numeric abilities or a bit of muscle power. Although there are some tasks which are high value activities and require limited skills, the general rule is that 80% of tasks require medium/low skills.

Thus we have a simple matrix.

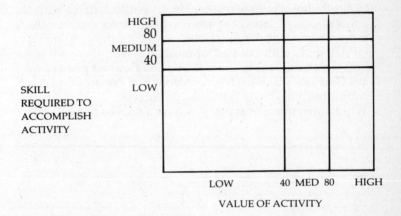

How do you spend your time? In lots of low value and low skill activity which would be represented towards the lower left of the diagram? Or in medium or high value skills and activities. If you apply the third principle and do only those tasks which no-one else can or should do, then you should find yourself moving steadily into the effective top right hand corner of the matrix.

Have a look at your list of daily activities (page 34). Look down the list for high value/high skill activities. My experience suggests that you will not have many — only one in five.

Focus on Success

You have probably attempted to organise your life before — by planning, daily action lists, flow charts but the demands of your responsibilities have meant, all too often, that the important has given way to the urgent. Your resolutions have been forgotten in the revolution which is the daily cycle; priorities have been reversed; targets have been undermined and your pathway has become littered with failed attempts to put first things first.

Whatever you decide to apply to your living as a result of reading this book, it will not prove easy. The fourth principle encourages you to focus on what works for you.

Look at what you have achieved. Too often you allow yourself to become discouraged by what you haven't done rather than taking satisfaction from what you *have*. Time management is a never-ending work and it is all too easy to devalue the progress made and the ground covered. Think positively and give yourself regular positive feedback. Look at your efforts and highlight, each day, your successes. This is particularly so with the big tasks — those targets which will take weeks and months to achieve rather than hours or even years. In the creation story each day ends with the task unfinished — and there are fewer things which depress us more than a half finished piece of work — yet God looks on what has been done and declares 'It is good!' — unfinished yes, but good. Focus on success.

Write down five things that you have achieved today.

1. _____

2. _____

3. _____

4. _____

5. _____

Review Regularly

This principle cannot be over emphasised. The complexity of the interacting forces which create time management problems is such that constant vigilance is required.

Maintain a regular evening review. Go over each day identifying those effective and efficient times during the past twenty four hours. Look for incidents which tell you something about the way in which you work effectively. When were you at your best? What did you do that created more space for your priorities? Note any situations which you should seek to avoid or be on your guard against in the future. Consider briefly your plan for tomorrow and list your priorities. Review regularly. Remember the pointers from Round Nine about review. One was that to be of value in the learning process, a review must be organic, that is, it must take account of what you are learning and it must result in changes in your behaviour.

Review as you go. Review before you are finished. Review while you can still influence the outcome. In this way review will become an attitude rather than an activity. Ask yourself is this the best way? Is this the best approach? Can I improve? In this way you can improve continuously.

Move Forward One Step at a Time
The danger of the big task is that we try to bite off too much at once. Effective time management is an on-going process. Those gains made yesterday enable you to move forward into new and more challenging areas today, but for many people the big task is just too daunting to begin. The web of constraints, the myriad distractions, are too much to tackle. 'Where do I begin?' 'I have no time to manage my time.' 'It's impossible.' 'I'll manage somehow.' These are all the cries of a person on the time-rack — being pulled all ways at once, all nerves engaged, all systems straining — and getting nowhere. If you want to break out, then start now.

Break that overwhelming task, that impossible challenge, down into manageable steps. Each day is a new horizon, each day a new peak.

Don't seek each day to manage your time: that's your life-time objective. Your daily task might be to attempt to reduce each phone call to a maximum of three minutes, or to write no letters more than one page in length, or to extend your own quiet time for thinking and planning by one minute a day for the next 30 days without extending your working day. Whatever it is, define it, break it down small, focus on it, achieve it, congratulate yourself and then move on to the next step. One writer on time management describes the task of being more efficient as like 'eating an elephant'. There is only one way to eat an elephant — one spoonful at a time!

You must enlist the support of those around you in your organisations, families, churches, clubs. Recognise your dependence on others. Re-establish that web of constraint as a web of support.

Share the Work
The second major reason for failure in the area of time management, after the absence of clear targets, is that people try to go it alone. You cannot improve your use of time without involving others. In Round One we looked at other people as being some of your opponents, while in Round Ten we saw how helpful others could be.

There are two ways of looking at the problem of others — first you can see them as barriers to be overcome, or second you can see them as potential sources of help.

Look at this diagram. It represents two opposing forces.

What needs to happen for A to move to the right? The answer is that A needs to be increased in order to overcome the opposing force B. But that requires more energy. There is another way, of course, which is that the force B is reduced!

Take your large task and make a list of all those people whose help you will need to complete it with the least expenditure of energy.

Your list should be in two parts, part one with the names of those whose help you can immediately enlist and part two, the names of those whose opposition could make your task more difficult. Make your list now:

Names of those whose help I could enlist:

1._____

2._____

3._____

4._____

5._____

Names of those whose hinderance I could do without:

1._____

2._____

3._____

4._____

5._____

Using your organic planning chart (page 79) prepare a plan for winning the support of those people who could make your task more difficult. Do that now.

Give Space to Others

To enlist the help of others requires you to be willing to trust them and give them space. You will defeat your own purpose if you spend time checking up on your helpers. If you wish progress reports then fix the time of these well in advance and forget about the delegated work until then.

Your helpers will feel stronger and more valued if you show your confidence in them and let them get on with the tasks that you have asked them to do.

Don't keep looking over people's shoulders. You will have seen boxing matches where some seconds constantly harrass their fighter with streams of advice from outside the ropes, this not only can distract the boxer but it can seriously undermine his self esteem and confidence.

Before you pick up the phone, walk down to their office or pop into the garden to see how they are getting along, ask yourself — 'Is there something else that I could do?' If the answer is 'Yes', then do it! If the answer is 'No', — then sit where you are and practise your breathing for a while.

Stop When You Have Finished

You won't, of course, know when you've finished unless you've set clear targets. Avoid the never-ending task. In the creation story when the six days were over and the task complete we read that 'God rested'. I have emphasised the importance of taking time off when the job is done.

Statements such as 'being a better parent' or 'improving my time management' are traps; they lock you into what I call the 'hamster-habit' — engaging in tasks that have no clear end. Avoid them, for they will exhaust you mentally, physically, and spiritually.

Legend and folklore of many nations are filled with characters condemned to endless labour. When set responsibilities are going to be part of your life for a number of years, then make sure that you know what your next step is going to be. Always include these large tasks in your annual review and set clear targets for progress in the coming period.

A housewife came to me recently with a problem — housework! She had three children and a tired, untidy husband.

'Each day,' she explained, 'is the same long round of house chores — tidy, wash, hoover, polish, tidy, wash, hoover, polish ... I cannot stand it any more! It's never-ending.'

Her distress is a common feature of today. It affects not only those at home but also those whose responsibilities are routine and predictable. How can you break out of the repetition? The answer is to vary your horizons.

I recently met a shepherd on the high moor near my home.

He is often there, in the same spot, with a small leather and brass telescope, scanning the heather-clad hills and hollows.

In the way of someone born and bred in the city, I asked, 'Are you looking for some sheep?'

He continued to search for a moment longer then, without lowering the eyepiece, he replied, 'No. Just one.'

What was for me a large, widely scattered flock was for him an intricate pattern of families: mothers, daughters, sisters, cousins. He knew them all. Instead of seeing several hundred white, free-range sheep, he looked at each one, noting the unique features that were lost to me. He could focus and find meaning.

How do you work and think as the shepherd did? How do you deal with the endless, routine tasks? Here is what to do.

1. Break down the task, eg housework, into small parts. The shepherd did not see the whole flock at once.
2. Look in detail at each item that you handle. Come alive to the colour, texture, shape, colour, and sounds which are unique to each room, drawer, vegetable, or piece of paper.
3. The more tedious your task, the smaller and shorter should be your targets. So do not set 'to tidy the house by 11 o'clock' as a target if you find this is frustrating. Instead, set targets for each room.
4. Introduce variety by altering the sequence in which you tackle the work. Use all the freedom you have to choose what to do and when.
5. Keep a record of your progress.

Do these and you may rediscover meaning and satisfaction in every chore. You will avoid the trap of the never-ending task.

Follow Up

This is the last of the ten principles for good time management. Be alert to the signals that something is wrong: unexplained delays; excuses; or just that sixth sense which tells you all is not well. Check immediately: you may be the only one who can and should help and stay sensitive to your own condition.

Listen to your own inner rhythms. Do you feel rushed? Is your sleep disturbed? Be alert to bodily signals of bad time management — tension, irritability, poor concentration, tiredness — and act quickly to gain control.

Watch out for those surprises, like the anniversary or birthday that is today or — worse — was yesterday!

Watch for the intrusion of other people's priorities into your own.

Note that uncomfortable feeling that comes when you are not giving enough time to important areas: family, self, relaxation ...

Interval Training Exercises

Heavyweight learners
Identify a major task which you have as yet not approached in a structured way, and prepare an organic planning chart for it. (See Round Five, page 79).

Middleweight learners
Identify your high value/high skill activities from your daily time analysis completed in Round One, page 34.

Lightweight learners
This evening take a piece of fruit or a vegetable and examine it in detail for three minutes. Write down a full description of it and replace the item in the bowl or basket. Give someone your description and ask him or her to find the piece described.

Round Fourteen
Learning Your Lessons

In the Weigh-in you identified your learning weight — light, middle or heavy. Whatever your weight, there are some lessons which are harder to learn than others. For some of us vision building is difficult: our mind does not seem to work that way. For others of us it is no problem: our heads are full of visions; we just cannot get into action! But in all the areas of living we have the opportunity to learn. Go back now to the Pre-fight Check List and for each of the 36 statements, ask yourself this question: Do I now know what to do if I wish to change that? Do that now and count the number of times you can answer, 'Yes'.

If you have thirty or more, your investment in this book has been very worthwhile. Twenty or more and you have done well. Below twenty probably means you have not been doing the exercises! But no matter what your score is, you need to practise all the new skills that you have developed.

Taking the Time to Learn

At the heart of this book has been the need to review. Pilots take regular flight checks to ensure that their standards are maintained. You also must seek to maintain your disciplines. Midway through the fight, in Round Eight, we looked at review. A corner stone of that was the annual review day. In my experience, it will require you to have three of these before you really begin to find out how powerful a tool a review day is for improving performance and helping you to identify your lessons.

That means a three year programme of experimenting with and testing out the ideas in this book. There are no short cuts. Benefits you will have already, but do not settle for second best. Commit yourself to the three year discipline.

No book can cover the infinite variations of lives that go to make up the richness which is our society. But you have been given the tools to help you learn and keep on learning and you will do so, if you keep asking, 'What seems to work for me and why?' Use your 'high-high' group to give you more insights into your strengths and weaknesses. Teach yourself to live more effectively day by day, year by year.

Watch those around you. Note how they manage or misuse their time. Learn from them what to do and what not to do.

Aiming for Quality Time

As you improve your use of time, you will be tempted to misuse the time gained, wasting it on unimportant and unprofitable activities. The challenge is not to do more things with your time, but to increase the value of what you do. Emerson reminds us that we may ask for long life, but 'tis deep life or grand moments that signify.[36] The challenge then is to improve the quality of your use of time, to make your life's moments richer and of greater value to yourself and others.

Nor must you yield to the temptation to become time's slave. Time is given to you to serve you – so that you might achieve and mature within its bounds. Rabelais said, 'I never tie myself to the hours, for the hours are made for man, and not man for the hours.'[37]

There was a time when I thought that time management was about clock-watching. I've learned that it is not. I am just as late for as many appointments as I used to be! What has changed for me is the reason why I am late. Before I would be late because of bad planning. Now if I am late, it is because I have chosen to be, because what I was doing was more important than what I was going to do. My life is now governed by priorities, not by my watch.

But the temptation is always there to be forced back into that rut by someone else's machine.

Staying Open to Life

I am still learning, still discovering, because that is for me the nature of real living.

And tomorrow? Well tomorrow you and I will be different people: we will be older, we will have different memories, different opportunities and different lessons to learn. There are areas of my life which are targets for development, but not yet. I work on today's priorities, I consolidate yesterday's lessons and I prepare for tomorrow's lessons, whatever they may be. To achieve these three tasks I try to ensure that I am:

- open and honest with myself about my strengths and weaknesses.
- alert to what is happening to me now.
- considering the way that my dreams are leading me.

That way I can best ensure my success in the fight for effective use of time, and face the next round with confidence. These too are the disciplines that will help you mature in your fight for the effective use of your time.

Make a list of the things that you have learned in reading this book. Put them under the headings provided:

I have learned the following about myself:

a. My strengths

     1 _____

     2 _____

     3 _____

b. My weaknesses

     1 _____

     2 _____

     3 _____

c. My past

     1 _____

     2 _____

     3 _____

d. My future

     1 _____

     2 _____

     3 _____

e. The quality of my life

     1 _____

     2 _____

     3 _____

There may be other things that you have learned, for example, about people around you and their priorities and time problems. You will find it helpful to make a list of the priorities and time problems of the three adults most clearly associated with you. Do that now.

The three adults most closely associated with me are:

1 _____

2 _____

3 _____

Their priorities and time problems are:

a. Priorities

1 _____

2 _____

3 _____

Time problems

1 _____

2 _____

3 _____

b. Priorities

1 _____

2 _____

3 _____

Time problems

1 _____

2 _____

3 _____

c. Priorities

1 _____

2 _____

3 _____

Time problems

1 _____

2 _____

3 _____

Interval Training Exercise

You have checked your progress against the Pre-fight Check List. Your answers will tell you something about your strengths and weaknesses. Here is a short exercise to help you:

Focus on your learning. Complete the following sentence in ten different ways:

I am becoming . . .

1. _____
2. _____
3. _____
4. _____
5. _____
6. _____
7. _____
8. _____
9. _____
10. _____

Share your answers with your 'high-high' group.

Interval Training Exercise

Round Fifteen
Overcoming Your Enemy

At the beginning of the last round of any contest, the opponents touch gloves in recognition of the effort and time spent together in combat. It is a form of salute indicating that whoever wins, the battle has been worthy.

The Nature of the Enemy
Go now and look in a mirror. Perhaps you have one in your bag or case. If not, try to catch a sight of your reflection in a window or polished surface. You are your own opponent.

In her books *The Earth Sea* trilogy, Ursula le Guin's hero is Gad, the young magician.[38] His power and life are blighted by a horror that he knows he must face. In order to face it and win, he must learn its name, for in the naming of the enemy there is victory. In vain he searches for the secret of the name of the nameless foe, until at last he gains the great insight — he is his worst enemy; there is no greater foe than self — and in speaking his own name, Gad, he gains the victory.

Never lose sight of the fact that you are the greatest enemy in your fight for life — no one wastes your time as much as you do; no one steals your seconds as often as you do. You have been given the gift of life and time — no one can misuse them more than you.

Every morning as you wash, say 'Hi' to the arch time waster in the mirror — touch the glass in recognition of the one you have to beat — your foe will respond!

Although we looked in earlier rounds at those around you as important opponents, in the end — as in the beginning — I can state that time management is about life management, and life management is about self-management.

As you wake from your private world of sleep and rest, it is your skill, your determination, your energy and your environment which will influence your satisfaction with the coming hours. And as you retire to rest it is your attitude that dictates the level of peace you experience.

You are your enemy, but you can also be your healer.

And finally, do not lose sight of what this fight is all about. It is about living your life in a way that gives greater satisfaction, fulfilment and contentment. Each day is a new opportunity to win another round so that your everyday song will be an evening celebration of a round completed and won.

Winning the next round is your daily target. It is the target that you are engaged in right now.

There is no bell to end this contest. *Seconds Away!* is a call to begin, not to end. So as your fight continues, remember that he who governed the world before you were born shall take care of it likewise when you are dead. Your part is to improve the present moment.

Go to it, Champion!

Notes

[1] Robert J Burdette, 'The Golden Day'.

[2] Proverbs Chapter 29 v 18.

[3] William Shakespeare, *As You Like It* (Methuen & Co Ltd: London, 1975 [first printed, 1623]), Act II, Scene VII, line 163-6.

[4] Robert Browning, 'Rabbi Ben Ezra', *Browning: Poetry and Prose* (Rupert Hart-Davis: London, 1950), p 397.

[5] Ecclesiastes Chapter 3 v 1-8.

[6] St Luke, Chapter 15 v 11-32.

[7] A A Proctor, 'Now', *Stevenson's Book of Quotations* (Tenth Edition, 1974): 2020.

[8] Paul Tournier, *The Gift of Feeling* (SCM Press Ltd: London, 1981), p 5.

[9] Gordon MacDonald, *Ordering Your Private World* (Highland Books: Crowborough, 1985).

[10] St Paul's Letter to the Philippians, Chapter 4 v 13.

[11] Unknown, 'The Salutation of the Dawn'.

[12] Martin Luther King, August 28, 1963, March on Washington for Jobs and Freedom.

[13] St John, Chapter 19 v 30.

[14] St Matthew, Chapter 25 v 14-30.

[15] Peter Brierley, *Vision* (MARC Europe: Bromley, 1985).

[16] Simon Newcomb, quoted by J W Hayford in 'Why I Never Set Goals', *Leadership* no 1, Vol 5, p 46.

[17] William D Leaky, *ibid*.

[18] Abraham Maslow, *Motivation and Personality* (Harper & Row, Publishers: New York, 1954).

[19] Tim Severin, *The Brendan Voyage* (Hutchinson & Co Ltd: London, 1978), pp 95-96.

[20]Henry Wadsworth Longfellow, 'The Builders' (*Stevenson's Book of Quotations, op cit*), 2021.

[21]J Humble, 'Time Management: Separating the Myths and the Realities', *Management Review* (1980): pp 25-28.

[22]David Cormack, 'Making the Most of Your Team', *Seminar Notes* (MARC Europe: London, 1986), pp 24-25.

[23]David Cormack and Brian A Wallace, 'Revolution, Evolution and the Battle for Survival' in *People and Organisations Interacting*, edited by Aat Brakel (Wiley [John] & Sons Ltd: Chichester, 1984).

[24]Leslie Kenton, *Ten Day Clean-up Plan* (Century Hutchinson Publications Ltd: London, 1986), pp 83-115.

[25]Breathing exercise cassettes by R J Miller, *Relaxation* (Psychological Counselling Services, 80 Rosemont Road, Liverpool L17 6DA).

[26]Douglas Adams, *So Long, and Thanks for All the Fish* (Pan Books, Ltd: London, 1984).

[27]Stephen B Douglas, *Managing Yourself*.

[28]Richard Foster, *Meditative Prayer* (MARC Europe: Bromley, 1985).

[29]Audrey Livingstone-Booth, *Stressmanship* (Severn House Publishers Ltd: London, 1985).

[30]O W Holmes, 'Our Banker' (*Stevenson's Book of Quotations, op cit*): 2002.

[31]Charles Dickens, *The Personal History of David Copperfield* (Macmillan & Co Ltd: London, 1927 [first published 1850]), p 163.

[32]Charles Darwin, *On the Origin of Species by Means of Natural Selection* (Grant Richards: London 1902 [first published 1859]).

[33]Richard Bach, *Jonathan Livingston Seagull* (Turnstone Press Ltd: Wellingborough, 1972).

[34]Tony Buzan, *Use Your Head* (BBC Publ: London, 1974).

[35]Horace Mann (*Stevenson's Book of Quotations, op cit*): 934.

[36]Ralph Waldo Emerson, 'Works and Days' (*ibid*).

[37]François Rabelais, *Works* (*ibid*).

[38]Ursula K le Guin, *The Earth Sea Trilogy* (Penguin Books Ltd: London, 1979).

Index to Topics

Notes